£15
Signed

July 2008

BALLYMENA

CITY OF THE SEVEN TOWERS

To Michael

Looking Forward to
working once again
with OBP!

Nicola

NICOLA PIERCE is a freelance writer, who has co-written
The Last Executioner, *Angel of Bang Kwang* and *Ms Bangkok*
all of which are published by Maverick House.

STEPHEN STEWART is a Ballymena-based freelance photography, who
specialises in landscape and architectural photography in Northern
Ireland. You can check out his work at
stephenstewartphotography.co.uk

BALLYMENA

CITY OF THE SEVEN TOWERS

Nicola Pierce

Photography by
Stephen Stewart

Waterstone's

Published for Waterstone's Booksellers Ltd in 2007 by The Brehon Press Ltd
1A Bryson Street, Belfast BT5 4ES, Northern Ireland

Text © 2007 Nicola Pierce
Original photography © 2007 Stephen Stewart

Additional photography on pages 27, 31, 35, 39, 43 and 47 is reproduced by
kind permission of Ballymena Borough Council.

ISBN: 978 1 905474 19 6

Design: December Publications
Printed and bound by J H Haynes & Co Ltd, Sparkford

CONTENTS

Acknowledgements 7

PART ONE: HISTORY 11

PART TWO: PEOPLE 51

PART THREE: SPORT 127

PART FOUR: GHOSTS 143

Suggested Websites 153

Bibliography 155

Index 157

ACKNOWLEDGMENTS

The author would like to thank the following people for their help in making this book possible:

Broy De Barr, from the Ballymena Museum, was extremely helpful in sourcing and providing old photographs;

Damian Keenan and Brendan Anderson at the Brehon Press went, as usual, above and beyond the call of duty;

Stephen Stewart made himself available, at ridiculously short notice, to take the beautiful photographs that are "strewn" throughout the book;

Paul and Jake at December Publications performed miracles under pressure;

Roger White, the manager of Waterstone's in Ballymena, offered absolute support from the start.

For my parents
Nicholas & Breeda Pierce

PART ONE
HISTORY

THE NAME BALLYMENA HAS UNDERGONE quite a few transformations, in terms of structure and spelling, in its earliest history: *Ballymenagh*, *Ballymanagh*, *Ballimin*, *Ballinmanaghar*, *Ballymenoch* and *Ballymineagh*. However, it is generally agreed that the name means "Middletown" or "Middlemosttown", which refers to the geographical fact that the town is, more or less, the central point of the county of Antrim.

According to a collection of articles which began in the *Ballymena Observer*, on 22 August 1857, there used to be a standing stone, nine feet long and 34 feet wide, that might have been specifically erected to mark the *exact* centre of Antrim. It had long been a mystery as to who had put it there and in what year. It couldn't be missed; it stood entirely alone in the middle of a field, a long way away from any other type of rock or stone. Unfortunately, this field was part of lands given over to the Union Workhouse and when the contractors moved in to start building, a workman took it upon himself to blow up the stone, thus clearing the field of its protruding obstacle.

UNSUSPECTING TOURISTS COULD EASILY PASS through Ballymena on their way elsewhere and not realise the wealth of history that the town is steeped in. We know that Saint Patrick began his herding duties on Slemish sometime throughout 401AD but the first record – or at least, the earliest known record – of the area dates from 480 when early Christian communities were founded at Connor, five miles south-east of Ballymena, and at Kirkinriola, two miles north.

Ringforts were also found in the townland of Ballykeel and a site known as Camphill Fort, in the townland of Ballee, may also have been of this type.

Ringforts were basically what you would assume them to be: rings or circles of ground surrounded by a ditch, or mound of dirt or stone. They have a variety of names, *ráth*, *dún*, *lios*, rath and fort. Stone examples are known as cashel (*caiseal*) or caher (*cathair*). There are more than 45,000 in Ireland, making them the most commonplace of archaeological monuments.

In Kirkinriola there is evidence of the ancient parish church and graveyard, including a souterrain, which was an artificial underground structure, made from either stone or wood, usually found near ringforts. Large trenches were dug out and then roofed over. They had two possible functions: they made excellent cupboards, or storage facilities, because they were mostly dry if a little cold; and secondly they would have been used as hide-outs in the face of marauding foreigners. Some of them came with quite a few extras in the form of hidey-holes, if the souterrain had more than one level; secret passages, guard-chambers, ventilation shafts, drains, and even paved floors were to be found in some trenches.

In 1868 there was great excitement when a local gravedigger found a large slab of stone on which was carved a cross with the Latin inscription, *ord do degen*, referring to Bishop Degen, who lived in Ireland in the seventh century. You can see this stone for yourself in the porch of the Parish Church of Saint Patrick, in the parish of Kilconriola, Castle Street, Ballymena.

Then, in 831, Connor, which was still a tiny village, was ransacked by Danish intruders, led by the fierce Thergest, when they sailed up the River Bann to Lough Neagh. They burned the church to the ground and pretty much anything else that stood out. There was another invasion in 1177 when three hundred Normans arrived, under the leadership of John de Courcy, and took over the Kingdom

Harryville Motte

of Ulidia, from Carlingford Lough all the way to the Bishop's Causeway. There's no definite conclusion regarding the parents of John de Courcy but it is generally believed that his family owned property in Somerset and Cumbria. The invading army was accompanied by Henry II's deputy, William fitz Audelin. They made their stamp on the landscape by erecting huge mounds of earth on which were built wooden towers, known as mottes. Harryville's motte-and-bailey is one of the best examples in Northern Ireland, while others can be found at Camphill and Ballygarvey, although some scholars believe that Mid-Antrim's motte-and-baileys were built by Irish clansman who merely copied the invaders' work. In 1177, and again in 1178, the O'Flynns defeated the Earl of Ulster, John de Courcy, in a series of battles.

Less than two hundred years later Edward Bruce, whose brother was King Robert I of Scotland, better known as "Robert Bruce", invaded Ireland. Five miles south of Ballymena the great Battle of Tawnybrack took place on 10 September 1315, when Edward's army confronted and beat the Norman Earl of Ulster Richard De Burgo's forces.

In 1576 Queen Elizabeth I granted land, including the town of Ballymena, to Sir Thomas Smith, who brought English settlers over to make their homes there. There was a condition to this grant: Sir Thomas was to arrange one soldier for every "plow-land" and one "horse soldier" for every two "plow-lands", so that there would be an army who could be brought together within fifteen days to serve anywhere in Ulster under Her Majesty's Viceroy.

> *Whereas there hath been, in her Highnesses Earldome of Ulster, divers parts and parcels that lyeth waste, or else inhabited by a wicked, barbarous, and uncivil people – some Scottish, some Irish wilde – such as lately were rebellious to her Highness.*

The land had been given to the Crown after Shane O'Neill's resistance in the previous decade. By 1581, however, Smith's settlement had failed after he neglected to maintain the stipulated soldiers, and the land reverted to the Crown again until 10 May 1607, when King James I granted the Ballymena estate to the native Irish chief Ruairí Óg MacQuillan. Several owners later and the land became the home, and possession, of William Adair, a Scottish laird from Kinhilt in southwestern Scotland. Naturally there is a bit of a story to explain how this came about.

The Adairs

It was about 1380, a mere seven years before Chaucer published his *Canterbury Tales*, and a Robert Fitzgerald owned lands around Adare in the south of Ireland. Amongst other things, he battled and defeated the "white knight", a distant cousin of his. Despite Robert's father being the Earl of Desmond, the son wasn't considered a nobleman; therefore it was absolutely outrageous for him to slay a knight. Trouble flared for him almost immediately and he was forced to flee Ireland for the relative safety of Wigtownshire in south western Scotland. He prudishly decided to change his name just in case he was followed and took the name Adare, in place of Fitzgerald, after his previous home.

Always on the look-out for adventure, Robert heard that the King of Scotland had placed a bounty on the head of a man called "Currie", a well-known thief and pirate. The thief lived in an impressive castle that was virtually impossible to break into and the King promised this impenetrable fortress to whoever brought him Currie's head. Robert decided that would be him and set about staking out the grounds until he sighted the owner. He was rewarded one evening, and followed the pirate until it was safe to invite him to take part in a duel, which Robert won, beheading the corpse at Colfin Glen. The story goes that when Robert brought the head to the King's court one of the Royal courtiers asked, "Who dared encounter Currie?" and Robert duly replied, "I dare!" "Good," declared the King, "let that always be your name." Currie's head actually adorns the Adair crest. Robert took over the thief's castle and became known as Adare of Portree, which means "the King's port". His proud descendants built a castle, which they named Kinhilt, to mark the spot where he took Currie's head.

Many, many years later, in 1608, the Adair descendants exchanged Dunskey Castle for lands in Ballymena that were owned by Viscount Montgomery of Ardes. They moved over here but kept Kinhilt until approximately 1690, the year of the Battle of the Boyne between King William III and the former King James II. Robert Adair raised a regiment of foot soldiers along with sixty horses for the victorious King William and the Protestant cause. He was rewarded for his services with a knighthood. Had King William lost, Sir Robert would have lost in turn his estate as it was on the list of Protestant-owned properties to be confiscated by James II and the parliament he had convened in Dublin.

In 1626 Charles I granted William Adair a Charter to hold two annual fairs and a free market at Ballymena every Saturday forever more. Henceforth the Adairs began to prosper, as did the little town. William Adair was true to his word, so much so that the market continued in Ballymena right up until the Thomas Street site was transformed into the Fairhill Shopping Centre not too long ago. The original Charter continued to be held by the Borough Council.

THERE WAS STILL A LOT OF STRIFE to be got through. In 1641, the local Ballymena garrison fought against the Irish Roman Catholic rebels but had to retreat to Carrickfergus. Stories of massacres and bloodshed abound from this era and it would appear that nobody was spared, no matter what age or gender. A local man, Walter Kennedy, was head of the garrison at Clough, north of Ballymena,

Galgorm Castle

which was stationed at the Oldstone Castle that was built by the McQuillans. Over a hundred terrified locals were hiding out in the castle from the rebels. When the place was surrounded and there was a call to surrender, Kennedy made the brave decision to comply on the condition that the refugees would be let go free. It appeared to him that a deal was struck and his men laid down their arms. But he was deceived. The rebels imprisoned the soldiers in the castle while the aged, women and children were told they could make their way home. A first group, of maybe twenty or more, started on their journey but they didn't get far, being heinously butchered just outside the castle. The second group of unarmed locals, perhaps oblivious to the massacre outside, set off together but they too were slaughtered: defenceless old men frustrated by their useless bodies, frantic women having to watch their children being run through with swords before being killed themselves. An awful long four months later the inmates were released from the castle thanks to the Marquis of Antrim who arrived from Slane on 30 April 1642.

As an interesting aside, London was also having a miserable time of it. In 1665 a whopping 75,000 succumbed to the Great Plague and, just a year later, the Great Fire of London swept through the city bringing another large loss of life.

Ballymena's first market house was built in 1684, on what today is the present town hall. It was either inside or right in front of this building that merchants of all kinds set up their stalls. There were covered archways which sheltered the stalls in wet or blustery weather. There was also a proper, and public, "weigh-bridge" of weighing scales so that the customers could be sure they were not being cheated by paying more for less. The upstairs of this building served several purposes: it was a general meeting room for the townspeople, and it was also a court room used by the Justices of the Peace. The building also housed the town's fire alarm, a bell which could be heard throughout the vicinity.

In 1690 the Duke of Württemburg, a supporting general of King William, used Galgorm Castle as his headquarters. This was around the time that Robert Adair raised a Regiment of Foot for King William III and fought for his king at the Battle of the Boyne.

In 1707 Ballymena received its first Protestant parish church, 120 years before its first modern Roman Catholic Church was consecrated.

The castle that James I had built in Ballymena in the early seventeenth century was burnt to the ground in 1740.

St Patrick's Church
The original parish church of Kilconriola was destroyed during the Reformation. In 1707 building started on a new church which was consecrated 14 years later in 1721. Today the tower, which is all that remains of this chuch, stands in Church Street. It was decided that a bigger church was needed for Ballymena's growing population and so it was decided to replace this second church with one that could seat 800 people.

In 1853 the foundation stone for St Patrick's was laid appropriately enough on St Patrick's Day. The Adair family presented the site for the new church and made a huge contribution to the building costs of £5,000. Rector William Reeves oversaw the project and it was consecrated just two years after the foundation stone was put in place. How could the Rector have known that the first funeral to be held in St Patrick's would be that of his wife, who died giving birth to their tenth child? A window on the north aisle is dedicated to her.

Disaster hit the church when it was destroyed by fire on 13 December 1879 but it was a temporary setback. Within 15 months the church was completely rebuilt by the same contractor who had built the original and it was also re-opened by the same bishop who had consecrated it in 1855.

The Bell Tower is over 90 feet long, making it one of the highest points in Ballymena; it was one of Lord Waveney's seven towers.

There is a plaque on the outside wall of the tower dedicated to William Reeves. He was also the headmaster of the Diocesan School – the forerunner of the present Ballymena Academy.

The Gracehill Moravian Settlement

In 1457 the Protestant Moravian Church was established in Bohemia, an area which later became known as the Czech Republic. The church believed in unity and freedom in doctrinal thinking, believing that Jesus Christ was the basis of everything. Being a good Christian was a common goal and reflected in the church's motto: "In essentials, unity, in non-essentials, liberty, and in all things, charity."

The Moravian settlement at Gracehill, the only full scale Settlement built by the Moravians in Ireland, was largely down to John Cennick, a friend of John Wesley. The followers of John Hus – the Rector of Prague University, who lost his life after his public criticism of the Catholic Church in 1415, when he was burnt at the stake – travelled far and wide, bringing his teachings about a united brethren to the Americas, the Caribbean and Africa. They arrived in England in the early eighteenth century and took part in the Evangelical Revival, impressing John Wesley, the founder of Methodism, and his colleagues with their goodwill and eagerness to connect with all mankind under the term of "Christianity".

Sometime in 1746 John Cennick was in Dublin preaching about the Moravian's *Unitas Fratrum*, "Unity of Brothers", when he was approached by a merchant from Ballymena, Joseph Dean, who invited Cennick to speak in his hometown. Cennick, a tireless worker, agreed and travelled north a few days later where his initial listeners numbered maybe twelve or so. However, in a matter of days, the word spread and Cennick quickly found himself addressing crowds of 2,000 or more. A new religion, or a new way of thinking,

Gracehill Moravian Church

can be a terrifying thing for some people and, while Cennick was converting many new supporters, he was also making enemies. A short while later he beat a hasty retreat from Ballymena after his life was threatened. For now he was gone, but it was not forever. Two years later, in 1748, he returned to continue what he had started. He settled in Crebilly and took to the road, preaching in and around the Ballymena area. He moved to Gloonen, between Ahoghill and Gracehill, a year later.

By all accounts Cennick suffered greatly throughout his early days as a preacher in England. He spent five years in Wilshire giving sermons in the face of sometimes brutal opposition. On a good day hecklers would only try to drown out the sound of his voice by beating pots and pans, or by encouraging dogs to howl by swinging a cat in a cage over their heads. On a bad day they beat Cennick, or dumped him into dirty ponds, or threw dead dogs at him. But it didn't matter what they did; he never stopped working, whether travelling to preach, working on the land, or writing speeches late into the night. Not surprisingly he succumbed after years of burning the candle at both ends. While travelling to London he caught a fever and died, at only 39 years of age, leaving behind a wife and two children. He is buried in the Moravian cemetery, Sharon's Garden, in Chelsea, England.

His legacy thrived in Ballymena despite his premature passing. In 1759, four years after Cennick's death, land in Ballykennedy, just off the road between Ballymena and Ahoghill, was leased and then later bought from Lord O'Neill. This was the beginning of the Gracehill settlement. Accommodation was built around a church which then spread out in a large square. Aside from family dwellings there were communal houses for single men, single women and widows. There were also boarding schools for both genders. The church had two separate entrances for the two genders and this separation also translated to "God's Acre", or the burial ground. Men were buried to the left and women to the right of a central path. Since Moravians believe that everyone is equal in death each headstone is the same size and design. There was also a farm, a shop, and an inn which provided further accommodation. The settlement, with its precise layout and Georgian architecture, was the first place in Northern Ireland to be named a conservation area.

MEANWHILE, FROM THE 1730S, Ballymena began to make a name for itself as an important linen market. By 1783 the town was one of the nine leading Ulster markets for the sale of brown linen, with sales of £100,000 in that year alone.

The *Belfast News Letter*

The *Belfast News Letter* has the unique honour of being the oldest newspaper in the whole of the English speaking world, and it was founded in Ballymena! The paper manufacturer, Francis Joy, set up the paper in 1737, eighteen years before Samuel Johnson published his dictionary and just five years before Christopher Columbus found America. These first editions were printed in the form of a letter, no longer than two pages. The earliest copy in existence is from Tuesday, 6 March 1730, and includes reports from Hungary, Germany, Denmark and France – quite a feat when one considers the labour involved in international travel and communication then.

An interesting aside: the rebel Henry Joy McCracken was the grandson of the founder of the *News Letter* and his execution for his part in the 1798 rising brought great sadness to his family.

Later, the paper was moved to Randalstown before making its permanent home in Belfast.

The *News Letter* claimed its very first world exclusive when it published the first copy of The American Declaration of Independence to be seen outside America. Thanks to atrocious weather off the north coast of Ireland the ship carrying one precious copy of the Declaration for King George II was forced to pull in at Derry. There it was met by a horseman who couriered the document to Belfast where it was to be put aboard another ship that was bound for England. Unfortunately we don't know exactly how the *News Letter*'s editor got his hands on the Declaration but he did and it resulted in a jubilant front page on 23 August 1776.

The following century, in 1871, the *News Letter* had another world exclusive, when it began printing the world's first regular news feature for women.

Among the events the paper covered were the trial and execution of the infamous Dick Turpin in March/April 1739; the natural disaster that was the potato famine and the dire consequences for the Irish population, including mass emigration; the penal laws and the discrimination against the Catholic and Presbyterian communities.

Before the partition of Ireland, in 1922, the *News Letter* was an all-Ireland newspaper distributed all over the island. After 1922 it became a northern newspaper with a predominantly unionist political perspective.

The paper has been a reliable and constant source of information for over 272 years, despite the chaos caused by the Troubles. When over twenty-one staff were injured in an explosion near its premises it still didn't prevent the newspaper from reaching the stands.

The 1798 Rebellion
The French Revolution had taken place in 1789 with the storming of the Bastille in Paris. Four years later King Louis XVI and his wife, the infamous Marie Antoinette, were executed to the delight of the French lower classes. Hostility for the rich and the monarchical system spread throughout Europe over the next few years, along with the desire for "liberty and equality". Irish people were inspired by the French to dream of a democratic government in place of the English Royal Family. Others dreamt of the seizure and re-distribution of

St Patrick's Church

wealth, so that it could be shared equally amongst all men. There was a sometimes fragile army made up of Catholic and Protestants, encouraged by local parish priests and clergy. In the summer of 1798, on 7 June, Ballymena was stormed and taken over by 10,000 United Irishmen. This assault was led by Belfast man, Henry Joy McCracken, who ordered his followers to seize their local towns. Three local men, who were part of a group attempting to defend the Market House from the intruders, were killed in the ensuing battle.

Ballymena man, James Raphael, was one of the three killed. The defenders were small in number compared to the 10,000 men they faced, and the story goes that, when they quickly ran out of bullets, they tore the buttons from their jackets to shoot at the attackers. James was killed by a cannon ball that was fired from his own house in Mill Street. When the fighting ceased, and it was safe to do so, James's body was removed by his brother to the latter's house in Galgorm. His remains lie with the other members of the Raphael family in the Old Graveyard at Kirkinriola.

A Galgorm woman was responsible for the eventual capture of the infamous rebel, Thomas Archer. A shoemaker from Ballymena, Archer got caught up with the United Irishmen and wasn't ready to forego the fighting life once the rebellion had come to an end. He and his gang of friends carried on their own campaign with, initially, patriotic motives of disarming and "converting" loyalists to the "United" cause. Unfortunately it was hard to stay on the straight and narrow as a gang on the run from the Crown and pretty soon they were wanted for thieving and, perhaps inevitably, the murder of a loyalist.

Archer took shelter in a house in Galgorm but it proved a dreadful mistake. The woman of the house went to the authorities to inform them about her famous guest, after first wetting the gunpowder for his blunderbus. He was done for; arrested and then hanged from an ash tree in 1800. His body was placed in an iron cage and hung at Harryville Moat, where his poor parents could see it from their house, as a warning to anyone else who fancied their chances against the Crown. The wife of an officer wrote to her friend in England to say that her new home was very nice except for the disconcerting fact that Archer's body could be seen no matter where she took her daily walk.

BY THE END OF THE EIGHTEENTH CENTURY there were five streets in Ballymena: Castle Street, Bridge Street, Mill Street, Church Street and Shambles Street (now Linenhall Street), and they formed a cross to the north of the river, now the centre of the town. The residents numbered 800, which jumped to 3,000 over the next forty years.

In 1854, three years after the American writer Herman Melville published *Moby Dick*, a Board of Town Commissioners was set up under the Towns Improvement Act. Ballymena was growing in size and population and it was time to reflect that in the facilities. Accordingly, the Board brought in piped water and improved and lit the streets.

The *Ballymena Observer*

The *Ballymena Observer* first appeared in 1855 and was owned and edited by John Weir from 1886 to 1927. Just out of interest, 1855 was the same year that Nurse Florence Nightingale was tending to the wounded in Crimea. John was also responsible for the fictional character of Bab M'Keen. When he died his son William took over until 1946 when *his* son, Major Jack Weir, continued on with the family tradition.

The Weirs were also responsible for 65 editions, between 1889 and 1954, of the *Ballymena And Mid Antrim Almanac And Directory*, more popularly known as *Bab M'Keen's Almanac*.

Through the character of Bab the Weirs provided the *Observer* readers with up to date news items in the common briad Ulster Scots of the time, which Bab "spoke", thereby making him an historically important factor in the recording of the language.

Today the *Ballymena Times* is a direct descendent of John Weir's *Ballymena Observer*.

Ballymena Castle

In 1865 work started on the new home for Robert Alexander Shafto Adair. It was a new Ballymena Castle no less, built in the Demesne, near where the first Ballymena Castle had been built by James I and then burnt to the ground by the Normans. Work on the fancy abode wasn't finished until 22 years later. Built in the elegant Scottish baronial style, the castle was a prominent landmark and source of pride in Ballymena. This style of architecture was hugely popular for anyone with Scottish origins, and money. It was highly decorative, mixing architectural styles so that one building could end up looking like a cross between a Gothic church, medieval castle and a French chateau, with plenty of turrets, towers and fancy gables.

Unfortunately, Ballymena Castle would not last beyond the next century. About ninety years later the castle was demolished following a fire, which left an unsafe ruin in its wake. It was a relatively short life for a building of its kind. All that remains today are some of the charred stones, absorbed into the church hall beside Saint Patrick's Parish Church, which was built in the general location of the entrance gate to the castle.

Industrial and Commercial Life in the late 1800s

In 1891 a book was published on the industries of the north. Nine Ballymena businesses are included with the description of the town, populated by 9,000 around this time, as a busy centre of linen manufacturing with important spinning-mills, bleach-works and dye-works. It flax and linen market was also described as being "one of the most important in Ulster".

Ballymena Castle

The businesses listed with a brief summary were:

Robert Morton & Co., Flour and Oatmeal Millers, Ballymena.

Mr Morton receives high praise for his effective management of a business this size which employed fifty locals.

David McCartney & Son, Bacon and Ham Curers, Grain and Flour Merchants, Church Street, Ballymena.

The "Son", Samuel J. McCartney, was also a Justice of the Peace and an esteemed member of the Town Commissioners of Ballymena.

Kane Brothers, Engineers, Millwrights, Ballymena Foundry, Harryville, Ballymena.

The latest accomplishment of this firm was the fitting and installation of the machinery for the new weaving factory belonging to the Gault brothers.

Gault Brothers, Phoenix Weaving Factory, Ballymena.

A special mention is made of the fact that this new factory is lit entirely by "the electric light".

John Kane & Sons, Engineers and Millwrights, Iron and Brass Founders, Braidwater Foundry, Harryville Bridge, Ballymena.

Besides the usual engineering jobs, no other firm in the entire country did more in the way of cart axles than this one.

George S Wilson, Imperial Steam Mineral Water Works and Cordial Manufactory, Bridge Street, Ballymena.

Much is made of the fact that only the "purest ingredients" and the most "competent hands" were employed in this factory for the manufacture and distribution of a wide selection of refreshing drinks, including peppermint liqueurs, champagne nectar and tonic water.

John Gault, Prince Arthur Steam Sawing and Planning Mills, Ballymena.

This business was also a large importer of American and European timber, as well as Welsh slates and Chester tiles.

John Hanna, Dyer and Finisher, Kildrum and Lisuawhiggle, Ballymena.

Mr Hanna's company was so efficient and smoothly run, thanks to his procuring the latest machinery available for his plant, that it was said he remained unrivalled when it came to completing contracts "and works of any magnitude on the shortest notice".

Robert A Simms, Wholesale and Retail Draper, Merchant Tailor and Outfitter, The London House, Ballymena.

Apart from the general attractiveness of this most fashionable establishment Mr Simms was also lauded for the fact that he beat off stiff competition to win a three year contract to supply all the uniforms for the Belfast and Northern Counties Railway Company. Previously, this contract had never been carried out by the one firm.

ON 16 NOVEMBER 1845 the 10th Viscount Massereene cut the first clump of earth for the Belfast and Ballymena Railway. The engineer Charles Lanyon was employed to supervise the laying of the tracks, 38 miles in total, which was completed three years later. Ballymena's success and prosperity was believed to result from the Protestant work ethic and the legendary prudishness that its inhabitants had regarding money. And while there may be something in this, the importance of the railway cannot be discounted in connection with the growth of local businesses. By the end of the nineteenth century the Braidwater Spinning Mill, which employed around 1,000 people, was only one of several profitable linen companies. Do not forget that Ballymena was also a hugely important agricultural market, with something like 60,000 pigs being sold annually. The railway was a lifeline, bringing in materials and bringing out the goods to be sold elsewhere.

The Ballymena Workhouse

Even before the black days of the Irish potato famine there were thousands of hungry and penniless men, women and children barely surviving in the north. Apart from a handful of English charities and occasional well-meaning clergymen there was no support system in place for those who had fallen on terrifically hard times. Babies, children and young people were dying in their hundreds from the likes of small pox and typhoid.

The Irish workhouse system was created with the Work House Act of 1838 despite enormous opposition by the Irish Members of Parliament. The whole of Ireland, north and south, Protestant and Catholic, opposed the Bill. The Irish MPs presented a massive 86 petitions, comprising a grand total of 36,221 signatures, against the Bill, while just 593 signatures in favour were collected. It was passed regardless.

Parliament based the Act on the 1834 English Poor Law Amendment but, strangely, they left out one hugely important factor: whereas the English poor were granted the *right* to receive relief, the Irish poor were not. One of the Act's provisions was the creating of "Poor Law Unions" which carried out the administering of the Act to their relevant territories.

The Ballymena Poor Law Union was set up on 13 May 1840 to deal with an area of 252 miles. As with the rest of the country the Union's work was supervised by an elected Board of Guardians who

Ballymena Castle

met to discuss poverty related matters at 1pm every Saturday afternoon. Twenty-eight guardians represented Ahoghill, Ballyclug, Ballyconnelly, Ballymena, Ballyscullion, Broughshane, Clough, Cloghogue, Dundermot, Dunmanway, Dunminning, Galgorm, Glenbuck, Glenravel, Glenwhirry, Kells, Kirkinriola, Lisnagarran, Longmore, Newtoncromellin, Porgelenone, Slemish and Toome.

Building began on the Ballymena workhouse in 1842 on a six-acre piece of land north of the town. It was a typical design by architect George Wilkinson with separate wings for men and women. At the back of the main building there were additional rooms built, such as a bake-house, wash-house, idiots' ward, chapel and a dining room. The Guardians' boardroom was on the first floor, over the entrance and waiting room. Extra buildings were added to the workhouse to attempt to meet the demand during the Famine years of the mid-1840s.

The building was originally built to sleep 900 inmates. It cost £6,600, plus a further £1,800 for furniture and fittings. It was deemed to be ready for business on 3 November 1843 and admitted its first "visitors" two weeks later.

By 1846 the Ballymena workhouse was one of 128 built throughout Ireland. Within twelve months these houses were struggling under the weight of 115,000 starving poor. This was the height of the Famine, and the year became known as "Black '47". Conditions were desolate and the numbers of inmates only continued to rise; by 1851, there were over 215,000 people living in workhouses. Literally thousands would die in cramped and filthy conditions. Inspectors checked the workhouses but there was little to be done when, in one town, nearly 2,000 people were found living in a building that was meant for 800. There was no alternative on offer for the destitute.

During those bleak years Sir Shafto Adair turned over a house he owned to be made into a temporary fever hospital until a new separate building was built which could hold 40 patients. When people were weak from lack of food and nutrition, sickness and fever exploded and ran rife, picking off victims in their hundreds.

The workhouse later became the Braid Valley Hospital, with the old main building and fever hospital still standing.

The Seven Towers

Lord Waveney, formerly Sir Alexander Shafto Adair, was well known to the locals of Ballymena as he spent a large amount of his time in the area and would stop to chat with anyone he met. He must have been a colourful sight as he always wore his Glengarry cap and wrapped the rest of himself up in a check plaid. The story goes that he was showing Ballymena off to an English friend that he had invited over for a visit. They walked out the Old Coach Road to Ballymoney, which involved climbing a steep hill. There they stopped to admire the view of Ballymena. After a few minutes Lord Waveney declared to his companion, "There you see the City of the Seven Towers." It is assumed that they could see, in the following order, the towers of the Roman Catholic Church, the Episcopal Church in the old churchyard, the first Ballymena Presbyterian Church, the Episcopal Church in Castle Street, the castle, the Town Hall and the Braidwater Mill.

The People's Park

This popular spot was established in 1870, a gift from Lord Waveney to the people of Ballymena. The gate-lodge, situated at the Ballymoney Road entrance, shares the same architectural style that was preferred for the second Ballymena Castle, the romantic Scottish Baronial.

Lord Waveney actually designed the statue, "Armed Science", which stands in the park today. It isn't the original work; however, the marble original was exhibited at the Royal Academy in 1855 before being presented to the Royal Artillery Mess in Woolwich. The statue was sculpted by John Bell, a sculptor with links to the South Kensington based Department of Science and Art. "Armed Science" is an important allegorical work, making use of the two worlds of fine and industrial arts, and can be interpreted as an eighteen century snapshot on the ambiguities between art and warfare.

The Ballymena copy, made from terracotta, was unveiled two years after the park opened, by John Poynz, Earl Spencer and Lord Lieutenant of Ireland, whose future relative, Diana Spencer, would one day marry a prince.

The Town Hall

A raging fire in 1919 laid bare the first Town Hall, built on the site of the Market House. The post office, estate office and the caretaker's residence were also victims of the flames. Three long years went by without a proper venue for important business, official meetings and even social events. All meetings had to be held in the much smaller Protestant Hall, which was especially cramped during the Musical Festivals. Ballymena needed a new town hall. A competition was launched all over the United Kingdom, calling on architects to design the perfect building for a thriving, growing centre like Ballymena. The judging panel was presided over by Mr Kaye-Perry, the President of the Royal Institute of Architects in Ireland, and it was he who awarded the prestigious honour to the winning firm, Messrs. Jones & Kelly in Dublin. John Carson & Son, a Ballymena building and contracting firm secured the important tender while a Broughshane man, Samuel McTurk, was appointed clerk of works.

Before work could begin the old ruin had to be completely demolished, along with its prominent tower. Then, in July of 1924, His Royal Highness, the Duke of York, laid the foundation stone for the new building.

Braidwater Mill

The 20th Century

In 1900 Ballymena proudly assumed Urban District status with the first council meeting being held immediately, in January of that year. Thirty-seven years later the town became a Borough, a status it retained until the local government changes of 1973 resulted in the Borough incorporating the surrounding area of the Ballymena Rural District. There are nine villages around Ballymena: Ahoghill, Portglenone, Kells and Connor, Cullybackey, Glenravel, Clough, Moorfields, Gracehill and Broughshane.

Ahoghill

This large village is located to the west of Ballymena and it has been said that it was a town while Ballymena was still a pup. Sometime in the 1930s it became the first town in the Ballymena Union to get a proper sewage plant. It was also prone to flooding from the brook that eventually had to be diverted through the car park of the Brookside Church. Perhaps the worse case of flooding in relatively recent years happened on that awful morning of Sunday, 3 September 1939, the day that war was finally declared against Hitler's Germany. The locals feared that the end of the world was not too far away.

Portglenone

The village of Portglenone is located to the west of the River Bann on the Maghera Road. This location was an important factor in its growth as a settlement. There were two historic fording points at Glenone and Portnakim. The Norman invader John de Courcy had a castle built there in 1197 to protect the rites of passage between Antrim and Londonderry. His castle was part of a chain of castles that were built along the Bann from Lough Neagh to the sea.

As it stands on both banks the village is split between counties Antrim and Londonderry, with most of its residents living on the

Antrim side of the river. It was an industrious village with its grass-seed market, linen factories and salmon fishery. Timothy Eaton (*see* **People**) worked here before leaving for Canada.

Just outside the village, the Portglenone Forest Park is classified as an "Ancient Woodland" and is on the route of the River Bann which flows through it.

Kells and Connor

Not to be confused with the more famous Kells in County Meath, this village is south of Ballymena on the Antrim Road. There are, however, ruins of an early abbey, just some evidence regarding the antiquity of the place. It is twinned with the village of Connor, with which it has shared much of its history. In 1316 the Scottish Robert Bruce was crowned King of Ireland after a fierce battle in Connor, and then another near Kells.

Cullybackey

Now a large village to the northwest of Ballymena, Cullybackey once consisted of just one street called simply, but rather aptly, Main Street. Its most prominent landmark is the Cuningham Memorial Presbyterian Church which was completed around 1900. The church was erected by the Misses Cunningham in memory of their mother.

It's a strange name, Cullybackey, and there has been much debate over its original meaning: "The Woodland of the Birch Trees", "The Corner of the Spades", or "The Lame Dog's Leap" are just a few of the possible interpretations on offer with evidence to back them up. For instance, there are, and probably always have been, plenty of birch trees in the area. Furthermore, there is a tradition that a forge, which made the plates for wooden spades, stood on the site of the Cunningham Memorial Church. The spade-maker would have been an important, and busy, member of this rural community and his forge might have been a popular meeting place for the locals.

The site of the Presbyterian Church was certainly a favourite location. Sometime between the spade-maker and the Memorial church the site was the location for the "Sundialed Meeting House", which got its name from a sundial inserted into the wall with the inscription "John Wylie 1727". Wylie was one of the defenders at the Siege of Derry.

Cullybackey is also the ancestral home of Chester Alan Arthur, the twenty-first President of the United States, whose story is told in the **People** section of this book.

Glenravel

This village is known locally as the Tenth Glen, and covers an area from Martinstown to Parkmore. Its ancient history is evidenced by the standing stones and arrowheads found in the area. Meanwhile there is more than a hint to a link with Ireland's patron saint with the nearby Saint Patrick's Well. There are also plenty of Mass Rocks dating from the penal times when priests were forced to hold mass in secret throughout the countryside as it was against the law for Catholics to practice their religion.

Glenravel became a community of small farmers around the beginning of the nineteenth century. The Benn family were the first landlords and made a huge impact on the land with the planting of trees and hedges and the overall agricultural improvement.

Then, in 1866, James Fisher, from Barrow-in-Furness, opened an iron ore mine on the slopes of Slievenanee. Things would never be the same again. The fact that the rocks contained iron wasn't new information to the landlords Benn. Previously a Nicholas Crommelin had tried to smelt the ore in a furnace fired by local peat. However, it wasn't a success and he abandoned the project. His furnace can still be seen today near the village of Newtowncrommelin.

Meanwhile Edward Benn gave Fisher permission to dig his land for the next twelve months and charged him rent. Over the next six

First Ballymena Presbyterian Church

months 18,000 tons of iron ore was shipped to England where it was worth £1 a ton. Seven years later, in 1873, there were seven hundred men working in the mines while an army of horses, six hundred or so, was needed to cart away the treasure. This proved a slow process so there was much excitement with the introduction of a wire tramway which ran from outside Cargan to the Red Bay Pier. It was a pulley system, with full buckets of ore running down one side and empty buckets being returned on the other. Everyone was delighted except the men who had earned their living carting the ore with the horses. They directed their anger at the new system and pulled it apart. Unfortunately for them it was duly replaced in 1875 with something a bit more substantial, a railway between Ballymena and Parkmore.

The last mine closed in 1933; competition was too stiff against foreign ores being imported from abroad. There was a temporary resurrection during the Second World War when there was a shortage of aluminium for the fighter planes. Bauxite, the aluminium ore, was found with the Glenravel iron ore deposits. Business closed for good in 1945.

Clough

This little village is situated six hundred feet above sea level which makes it a good vantage point for splendid views of the surrounding valleys. It contains the ruins of an ancient castle and we can appreciate why. Thanks to its high location it would have been the perfect spot to build a fortress as it would have been almost impossible for an attacking army to sneak up on the castle's inhabitants.

Moorfields

Moorfields, which is more of a hamlet, can be found on the Larne Road near the breathtaking valley of the Glenwhirry River. The hills around the valley are huge, rising to well over 1,000 feet.

Gracehill

This small village was founded by the Moravian community between 1759 and 1765 and is the only settlement of its kind in Ireland. In 1975 it was designated a Conservation Area because of its Georgian architectural and historic origins.

Broughshane

The garden village of Ulster is three miles east of Ballymena, in the glorious Braid Valley, one of the gateways to the Glens of Antrim. The surrounding area includes Rathkeel and Buckna hamlets and the Oaklands and Tullymore Lodge Estates. There is also the Cleggan Lodge Estate in the Braid Valley. Today there are over 5,000 inhabitants spread between Broughshane and the valley.

Broughshane is renowned throughout the world for its many successes in competitions like Ulster in Bloom, Britain in Bloom, the European Entente Floral, and Nations in Bloom. The village is also the ancestral home of Sir George White, the hero of Ladysmith in the Boer War, who was awarded the Victoria Cross for his heroic role in the Battle of Charasia in India, and who was also knighted for military service in Burma.

IN 1805 THE ULSTER LINEN BOARD offered a subsidy to anyone who could set up a mill for spinning the substances hemp and flax, which were used in the manufacture of sails. This was the year that Lord Nelson defeated the French and Spanish in the Battle of Trafalgar. Four years later there were twelve mills set up across the counties of Donegal, Antrim, Down, Armagh and Tyrone, including one set up in Broughshane.

It would be churlish not to mention The Thatch Inn in the town. Nobody is entirely sure how old the pub is but in the 19 May 1789 edition of the *Belfast News Letter*, a piece advertises it under the name of "The O'Neill's Arms", describing it as "long established". In 1997 an old wooden street sign, dated 1773, was discovered which refers to the then landlord as being a Mr Thomas Peacock.

The Thatch is the only pub in Ireland to have its own brand of single malt whiskey, the "Podhreen Mare", named in honour of a triumphant racing horse and her master Charles O'Neill. The mare never lost a race in her glorious career and, on 7 June 1769, at the racecourse in Broughshane, she won yet again; however, the excitement of the event overcame her owner, who promptly collapsed and died after she passed the winning post. Charles's ancestor, Shane Mac Brian O'Neill, captured Broughshane (which means "Shane's Town") when it was known as Aghnaclare and it proved a favourite spot with his family. In 1865 his granddaughter, Lady Rose O'Neill, was granted permission by Charles II to hold a weekly market and two annual fairs in the village.

The Thatch received a royal recommendation in 1999 when H.R.H Prince Charles of Wales visited it for the second time and told waiting reporters that it was his favourite pub.

St Patrick's Barracks
Since 1937 these barracks have played host to generations of Irish soldiers starting out on a brand new military career. The Army requisitioned the area two years before Hitler's war finally broke out across Europe. It was ready in time to receive the Royal Ulster Rifles (RUR) from Armagh.

In the beginning the site consisted of five camps: Church Camp was located around St Patrick's Church and held German and Italian prisoners of war during the Second World War; Lowfield Camp was situated around HQ 107 Brigade and the sports fields; Highfield Camp mostly held army houses which held many young soldiers during the war; Castle Camp contained Ballymena Castle (before it burned down in the 1950s), which was used as the Officers' Mess and by the Women's Auxiliary Territorial Service and is now the site of the

Kilconriola Keep

Seven Towers Leisure Centre; and lastly the Demense Camp which became the St Patrick's Barracks we know today.

In 1959 the Royal Ulster Rifles (RUR) Depot was closed to allow new buildings and an overall refurbishment to take place. Its functions were transferred to a North Irish Brigade Depot in Eglinton. To mark the temporary closure the RUR crest was placed on the Clock Tower. Six years later the Depot re-opened and the foundation stone was placed at the foot of the Clock Tower.

Four years later it was decided to merge the regular battalions of the following three regiments: 1st Bn. Royal Inniskilling Fusiliers, who were stationed at Worcester; 1st Bn. Royal Ulster Rifles, who were stationed in Gibraltar; 1st Bn. Royal Irish Fusiliers stationed at Catterick. The date for the "re-birth" was set for 1 July 1968, when the three would become the 1st, 2nd and 3rd Battalions respectively of The Royal Irish Rangers (27th [Inniskilling] 83rd and 87th. A massive parade in Ballymena was held to celebrate the transformation of Headquarters The North Irish Brigade and The North Irish Brigade Depot into the Regimental Headquarters and the Depot of the new regiment. Field Marshal His Royal Highness The Duke of Gloucester, Earl of Ulster and Colonel in Chief of The Royal Inniskilling Fusiliers, became Colonel in Chief of the regiment.

In 1992 the Royal Irish Rangers merged with the Ulster Defence Regiment to form the Royal Irish Regiment (RIR Regt). The original RIR Regiment was formed in 1684 and then disbanded in 1922. Today you can visit the Royal Irish Regiment Museum in St Patrick's Barracks where its various weapons and uniforms are on display as well as a detailed history, beginning with the origins of the Inniskillings in 1689.

The Northern Ireland Training Regiment was formed in 2002 to provide training for soldiers from all of the Irish regiments. This training has recently been transferred to the Infantry Training Centre (ITC) in Catterick, Yorkshire.

St Patrick's Barracks is due to close in March 2008, the end of a 70 year old military presence for Ballymena. The Depot was a focal point for a variety of regimental activities in Ireland as well as recruitment and training.

Memorial Park

This beautiful park is just down from the train station on the Galgorm Road and holds Ballymena's War Memorial to the local people who gave their lives during the vicious conflict that was fought in the cold, muddy trenches of World War 1, trenches that stretched all the way from Switzerland to the English Channel. The obelisk lists almost 500 names of men from the Ballymena Urban and Rural Districts. Many of the Ballymena "regulars and reservists" fought in battles throughout the vicinity of the Belgian mining town of Mons as well as more obscure places where umpteen small-scale battles may not have made the headlines back home.

Anyone interested in discovering more about Ballymena's contribution to the war, or in tracing the career of a relative, should check out the website *www.freewebs.com*, a wonderful piece of work complete with the weekly updates from the *Ballymena Observer*, from 1914-1918, including accounts of wounded men and the dead, as well as the latest Ballymena recruits. There are also plenty of interesting stories, like that of Mr and Mrs Archibald McAteer, of 26 Waring Street, who bid farewell to their five soldier sons. Mrs McAteer actually received a letter from the King thanking her for her contribution.

The website also includes a "Virtual Memorial" which lists the dead alphabetically. Accordingly I was able to trace the McAteer boys and discovered that two of the brothers, Adam and Nathaniel, never made it home.

The Gibraltar Connection

In 2006 Ballymena was officially twinned with Gibraltar or "The Rock". Gibraltar's fiercely independent population of 27,000, of mostly Irish and Spanish descent, signed an agreement with Spain and Britain, after three centuries of ambiguity, for the right to choose their sovereignty.

During the Second World War a lot of Gibraltarians found themselves evacuated to eight wartime camps in Northern Ireland. Over a hundred were brought to Ballymena where they lived from 1943 to 1948 in nine specially built camps just outside Broughshane. Relations were built with the locals, some resulting in locals leaving Ballymena to return to "The Rock" with their new Gibraltarian spouses, while others saw Gibraltarians staying put in Ballymena after the war. On the fiftieth anniversary of the official withdrawal of the evacuees from Northern Ireland the Ballymena Borough Council erected plaques to commemorate this event as a tribute to the visitors and the contribution they made to the community.

Ballymena is also a sister city of Morehead, a small city in Rowan County, Kentucky, USA. The city was named after Governor James T Morehead and has a population of approximately 6,000. It's a hugely popular tourist spot as it's located in the foothills of the Appalachian Mountains and includes the Daniel Boone National Forest, where unlicensed hunting is allowed, but only with arrows instead of guns. The forest, a well-known conservation area, is visited by some five million people annually.

PART TWO
PEOPLE

Chester Alan Arthur

Throughout the seventeenth and eighteenth centuries emigration was an exciting and challenging prospective. Whole families took off to America in search of fortune, fame or just a new beginning. Ballymena made one of the more important contributions to this relatively new country when, in 1816, the family of Alan Arthur set off on their journey across the Atlantic. It must have cost a sleepless night, or three, to make the final decision to vacate the little cottage at Dreen, Cullybackey, and take a plunge into what must have been the unknown. However important a decision it was to Alan Arthur nobody, including himself, could ever have possibly imagined the massive consequences. His son, William Arthur, went on to become a clergyman and it was *his* son, Chester, born in Fairfield, Vermont, 5 October 1830, who grabbed the American dream with both hands.

Chester started school at Union Village in Greenwich, Washington County, where he proved a popular and diligent student. When he was eighteen years old he graduated from Union College and decided to study law, being admitted to the bar in 1854. He became a very successful lawyer, moving to New York to further his ambitions which now included politics. There he became a leading Republican politician. During the American Civil War he was engaged as engineer-in-chief, inspector-general and quartermaster-general of the state of New York; after the war he returned to his private practice.

Then, in 1871, President Ulysses S. Grant named him Collector of the Port of New York, a huge task that involved being wholly responsible for most of the customs revenue of the United States for the next seven years. He performed his job admirably and it brought him plenty of contacts and supporters, so much so that he was nominated for the vice-presidency in 1880. He took to the role alongside newly-elected President James Garfield until the following year when the President was assassinated.

Charles Julius Guiteau was a delusional religious fanatic who was enraged by his failure to obtain the post of United States consul in Paris, a job he had absolutely no relevant qualifications for. He took his revenge on 2 July when the President was out walking through the Sixth Street Station of the Baltimore and Potomac Railroad, now the site of the National Gallery. Garfield was on his way to make a speech in his alma mater, Williams College, in the company of the Secretary of State, James G. Blaine, the Secretary of War, Robert Todd Lincoln, and two of his sons, James and Harry.

When Guitea was arrested he shouted out, "I did it and I want to be arrested! Arthur is President now." This sensational statement led to Arthur being temporarily suspected of paying to have the President murdered. It is widely believed today that Garfield should have survived the shooting; one bullet grazed his arm while another was lodged somewhere in his spine, never to be found, although scientists now believe it was near his lung. His doctors made unforgivable errors: some inserted fingers that hadn't been sterilised into his wound to search for the bullet, and one doctor actually punctured Garfield's liver during the search. The inventor of the telephone, Alexander Graham Bell, had devised a metal detector, which was used to locate the missing bullet; however, nothing was detected since, unbeknownst to Bell and his advisors, the President was lying on a metal bed-frame.

Garfield spent the next few weeks bedridden and victim to one infection after another, which weakened his heart. In early September

People's Park

he was brought to the Jersey shore to see if the fresh air and isolation would help him recover from his injuries. It didn't. He died at 10.35pm on Monday, 19 September 1881. A massive heart-attack or a ruptured spleen, as a result of the shooting, was thought to be the cause of death. He was only forty-nine years of age and had been in office a mere four months. His remains were placed in a mausoleum in Lakeview Cemetery in Cleveland, Ohio. Six years later, a James A. Garfield Monument was dedicated in Washington.

Guiteau was found guilty of the President's murder despite his lawyers submitting a plea of insanity. He continued to insist that the President was dead because of his inept doctors and, while there may have been some truth in that, it wasn't a proper legal defence. Not surprisingly Guiteau received the death penalty and was hanged on 30 June 1882 in Washington D.C.

On 2 July 1881, Chester Alan Arthur was sworn in as America's twenty-first President. It had been a largely tense couple of months for Arthur since he was aware that quite a few people thought he was responsible for his predecessor's demise. At first he wanted nothing to do with the presidency and practically went into hiding for two months and eighteen days while the rest of the country held bated breath over Garfield's failing health. In the end he knew he had to fulfil his duty to his leaderless country and take the oath of office.

His immediate task was to bring calm and security to the troubled nation and his simple inaugural speech helped to do just that. Next he set about bringing in reforms to the civil service, in the form of the Pendleton Act, which he personally advocated and had established in 1883. He is probably best remembered for his transformation of the tattered navy; in fact, he was described as "Father of the American Navy" because of his passion in rebuilding it after the war. In 1882 Congress released money for the country's first all-steel vessels. This "white squadron" formed the basis of today's United States Navy.

President Arthur was a popular man who took on the biggest job in America at a particular turbulent time. He is fondly remembered for the fact that, for the first time since the Civil War, the White House represented dignity and stately hospitality. He was nicknamed "the Gentleman Boss" for his stylish clothes and love of fashionable society. He allegedly had eighty pairs of trousers in his wardrobe and it was said that he changed his clothes several times a day. When he took the office he voiced a few requests before moving into the White House – in short, a complete redecoration. This involved twenty-four wagonloads of furniture being removed from the House to be sold off at public auction. Arthur commissioned Louis Comfort Tiffany to replace these old pieces with new designs.

He had achieved such popularity that, on the day he left office, he was proposed to by not one, but four young women. However, he had sworn never to marry again after the death of his beloved wife, Ellen Lewis Herndon, twenty months before he was made President. It is said that he would not allow anyone to take any seat which would have been Ellen's had she lived to join him in the White House.

Mark Twain, the author of *Tom Sawyer* and *Huckleberry Finn*, was not fond of politicians in general but he did write that, "It would be hard indeed to better President Arthur's administration." This view was echoed by publisher, Alexander K. McClure, who wrote, "No man ever entered the Presidency so profoundly and widely distrusted, and no one ever retired... more generally respected."

Arthur died in New York on 18 November 1886, just over a year after leaving the office. It transpired that a year into his presidency he'd discovered that he had contracted Bright's Disease, a fatal kidney condition, but had kept the diagnosis to himself. He was buried next to Ellen in the Arthur family plot in the Albany Rural Cemetery in Menands, New York.

Today the Arthur Cottage is a popular must-see for visiting

Americans and proud ex-pats. It has been carefully restored and maintained by the Borough Council, and remains an important insight into family life in the 1800s, as well as a means to explore an incredible link that a tiny village near Ballymena has with the American Presidency.

Alexander Campbell

Alexander Campbell was born near Ballymena on 12 September 1788 to Thomas Campbell and Jane Corneigle-Campbell. Thomas was a minister in the Old Light Anti-Burgher Seceeder Presbyterian Church and would, like his son, become an early leader in the Restoration movement. Campbell Snr took responsibility for his son's initial education and wished to instill in Alexander a love for, and knowledge of, the classics: Latin, Greek, French, English literature and philosophy. He succeeded and Alexander went on to be a student at the University of Glasgow, where he developed a passion for the philosophy of the Scottish Enlightenment, in particular the works of John Locke.

More importantly Alexander was taught to question and challenge systems he didn't agree with; in short he began to question the rules and regulations of ecclesiastical doctrine. In May 1809, for the annual partaking of the Lord's Supper, Alexander was asked to take an exam to determine if he was good enough to participate in the proceedings. The service focused on the solemnity of Jesus' sacrifice on the cross, and the church elders were to visit all their members to confirm their worthiness. It could be a fearful time for the more tentative individuals of the congregation, who were usually the poorer elements. If a member was deemed deserving enough he was given a token to bring to the service, where he was to drop it into a plate at communion to show off that he had been officially declared worthy. The whole ritual disgusted Alexander, who believed that no man had the right to judge another's moral worth. As it turned out

"Armed Science" in People's Park

he passed the test and was handed a token, but when it was time to take communion he refused, returning the token to the elders, thereby breaking with the Church of Scotland, and any other church that declared itself to be the only way to reach God.

Meanwhile, his father was waiting for his family to join him in the United States of America. He had decided to make the journey in 1807 to combat ill health, a battle he decidedly won by living to the ripe old age of ninety. Just like his son he was working through serious doubts about his church's doctrine. The family were finally reunited in Pennsylvania on 19 October 1809. Once again his father undertook to direct his son's education and Alexander began an intense study of the Bible and theology in general.

What became known later as the Restoration Movement, or the Stone-Campbell Movement (which began in 1800), was based on the belief of equality, with a goal to banish divisions between Christians by returning followers to the New Testament, where the principles of "Truth and Union" could be found.

Two years later, on 4 May 1811, the Christian Association of Washington established itself as a church. Thomas Campbell was appointed Elder, Alexander was ordained as a preacher and four other deacons were selected. Their church – the Brush Run Church – was built two and a half miles from West Middletown of Pennsylvania.

On 12 March 1811 Alexander married Margaret Brown of Brook County in Virginia. After the birth of their first child Alexander began to think about the question of baptism. When Moses baptised Jesus he didn't just wet his head; Jesus' entire body was immersed in the river. After a lot of study on the subject, Alexander decided that total immersion was the Scriptural mode of baptism and looked for someone to immerse him. He found Elder Matthias Luce, a Baptist preacher, who agreed to perform the immersion after a simple confession of faith. On 12 June 1812, Alexander, his wife, both his parents and his sister, Dorthea, presented themselves to be baptised in the Apostolic Way. They were duly followed by the rest of their church members.

The following year the church expanded its flock by affiliating with the Redstone Baptist Association. It was important to connect and form a spiritual network with like-minded Christians. There was one condition to the affiliation: that the Brush Run Church would not be tied or limited in their teachings to the creeds of the Baptists. Alexander and his colleagues wanted to be free to teach their learned interpretations of the Scriptures. Not that this mattered to outsiders; the Brush Run Church was forever more considered to be a Baptist church no matter how individual its teachings.

In 1816 Alexander gave a sermon at Cross Creek in Virginia, which proved far too controversial for the Redstone Baptist Association. His "Sermon on the Law" was based on Romans 8:3: "For what the law could not do, in that it was weak through the flesh, God sending His own Son in the likeness of sinful flesh and for sin, condemned sin in the flesh." The Baptists believed in the equal importance of both the Old and New Testaments, while Alexander and his father emphasised the importance of the New Testament. Suddenly there were no more invitations to speak at Baptist gatherings. It wouldn't be until several years later that Alexander's teachings would find favour again, with another Baptist Association.

The Ballymena man was renowned for his evangelistic methods. He particularly loved a challenge, and displayed spectacular endurance when he sought to convert the popular atheist Robert Owen in a twelve hour argument that, while – allegedly –moving the non-believer to tears, didn't encourage him to advocate the notion of the existence of a god.

Alexander wrote several books based on his beliefs about Christian unity and the need to restore the true church that he believed was envisioned in the New Testament. He edited the Christian periodical *The Christian Baptist* from 1823 to 1830, the aim of which, he wrote, was to "espouse the cause of no religious sect, excepting that ancient sect called Christians first at Antioch". He then edited *The Millennial Harbinger* from 1830 until his death in 1866. This journal was hugely instrumental in the jump of Restoration supporters from 22,000 in 1830 to over 220,000 when Alexander died. In 1826 he published *The Living Oracles*, which was his own translation of the New Testament. It failed to attract much attention, however, even among the members of his own church. Alexander also wrote a few hymns, the most well-known being "Upon the Banks of Jordan Stood", as well as a hymnal which consisted of lyrics without music.

His most influential book was *The Christian System on the Remission of Sins* which put forward his belief that the ritual of baptism was solely for the purpose of the remission of sin. The book lays bare his frustrations at denominationalism: "In what more desolation is the kingdom of Jesus Christ! Was there at any time, or is there now, in all the earth, a kingdom more convulsed by internal broils and dissensions than what is commonly called the church of Jesus Christ?" Alexander believed that Christians could only be united using the words of the Apostles in the New Testament: "The union of Christians with the apostle's testimony is all-sufficient and alone sufficient to the conversion of the word."

He spent his final years in Virginia, where he founded Bethany College in 1840 to provide a more thorough education for ministers.

Ethna Carbery

Ethna Carbery was the pen-name of the Irish poet, Anna MacManus, who was born in Ballymena in 1866 to Belfast man Robert Johnston and his Donegal wife. Her poetry goaded the early Sinn Féin movement into a recognition and appreciation of the Gaelic culture. She was published in Republican periodicals such as *The Nation* and *United Ireland*. She was also a member of *Inghinidhe na hEireann*,

First Presbyterian Church, Ahoghill

which provided free classes in Irish, music, dance, history and drama and, it is said, inspired the poet W.B. Yeats to form the Irish National Theatre. With her close friend and fellow poet, Alice Milligan, she set up the monthly paper, the *Northern Patriot*, in 1894, as well as the *Shan Van Vocht* ("Poor Old Woman" – a pet name for Ireland) in 1896.

Charles Stewart Parnell had died five years previously, a broken man. Interest in Irish patriotism and history had seriously declined in the wake of the discovery of his long-term affair with the married Kitty O'Shea. He collapsed under the strain of the ensuing publicity, and from his efforts to communicate his position in person to as many people in the land as possible. Those who had once flocked to hear him speak now turned their backs on "the adulterer" as he travelled frantically around Ireland in often horrendous weather, trying in vain to remind angry townspeople and villagers that their priority should be their country.

Carbery and Milligan noted all this and decided to begin again, where Parnell had left off. This involved a huge amount of work: writing, editing, proof-reading, accounting, invoicing and corresponding to their world-wide subscribers. Every copy had to be folded up, addressed, and a few hundred stamps had to be licked on a monthly basis. The two women worked tirelessly without help, for three and a half years, so that patriots in Australia, England, France, India and South America could be kept abreast of daily events and filled with hope for the "Great Revival" of Irish art and literature. Readers were encouraged to send in their work. Carbery was particularly mindful of budding young writers and was always available for advice and plain old confidence-boosting. She did not search for fame or attention for her own poetry and writing; she merely used it as a tool, as something to stimulate others to try to achieve great things for their country. Love for Ireland was her motivation and she understood the importance of culture in establishing a nation's identity.

Her published works include *The Four Winds of Eirinn* (1902), *The Passionate Hearts* (1903) and *In the Celtic Past* (1904). In 1901 she married ex-teacher, poet and folklorist Séamus MacManus. The couple moved to Revilinn on the Eske estuary in Donegal, where she died unexpectedly the following year at the age of thirty-six.

One of her most popular poems was "Roddy McCorley", about the Protestant leader of the Society of United Irishmen who was executed on Good Friday in 1799 and – legend has it – is buried somewhere beneath the Belfast to Derry road.

Grover Cleveland

No less than 17 of the 41 American Presidents were either Ulster-Scots or had Ulster-Scots ancestry: Andrew Jackson, James Knox Polk, James Buchanan, Andrew Johnston, Ulysses S Grant, Chester Alan Arthur, Grover Cleveland, Benjamin Harrison, William McKinley, Theodore Roosevelt, Woodrow Wilson, Harry Truman, Richard Nixon, Jimmy Carter, George Bush and Bill Clinton. James Buchanan, who was the 15th President of the United States, is quoted as saying, "My Ulster blood is my most priceless heritage."

Grover Cleveland's family, like so many others, left their hometown of Ballymena in search of a better life in America. Grover was born in Caldwell, New Jersey, in 1837, the fifth of nine children to his Presbyterian minister father and wife. His father named him Stephen Grover after the first pastor of the Presbyterian Church of Caldwell, where he was Pastor at the time. Thanks to his father's profession, the family moved many times around central and southern New York State. When his father died in 1853 sixteen year old Grover had to forget about attending college as the family's finances were a priority. To support his mother he moved to New York City where he spent a year teaching at the state institution for the blind. Then, in 1855, he suddenly decided to try his luck in Cleveland, Ohio, where his uncle, a wealthy cattle breeder, hired him to manage his company. A year later Grover went on to study law in the offices of his uncle's friends, going on to making a name for himself as a lawyer in Buffalo, thanks to his single-mindedness whenever he was faced with a challenge of any description.

His uncle, an avid Republican, might have sparked the teenage Grover's initial interest in politics though he wasn't tempted to share his uncle's passions 100 per cent, becoming a Democrat in 1856 because he felt the party represented solid, conservative thinking. His interest in politics was further developed when he worked for the presidential campaign of James Buchanan. Buchanan went on to serve a single term as President and ironically enough, the next Democrat elected president, 30 years later, would be his junior staffer Grover.

During the American Civil War (1861-1865), when most men his age were in the Union Army, Grover managed to borrow money to pay a Polish immigrant to take his place in 1863, thereby dodging Lincoln's draft order. This practice was actually legal under the Federal Conscription Act and, inevitably, widely used by men of means. Grover later defended his actions by saying that he and his brothers had drawn lots to see who would stay behind to support his mother and four sisters.

It didn't take him too long to reach the White House. When he was 44 years old he became well known in political circles. In 1881 he was elected Mayor of Buffalo and later on he became Governor of New York. It was a mere three years later that he would receive the most noble and prestigious of promotions.

In 1884 the Republicans nominated James G Blaine for president which enraged reformation Republicans because Blaine had been publicly accused of accepting bribes from the railroads. These independent Republicans, nicknamed "Mugwumps", which meant "big chiefs", let it be known that if any Democrat cared to take on Blaine for the presidency he would receive their support – as long as he was an honest man.

Doorway of First Presbyterian Church, Ahoghill

The race was on. Grover's impeccable record was a magnet for the anti-Blaine crowd and, in July 1884, he received his nomination for president. Then the Republicans threw what they believed to be a massive spanner in the works. They found out that Grover may have fathered an illegitimate child when he was a lawyer in Buffalo with a Maria Crofts Halpin who may or may not have been something of a nymphomaniac. The lady in question was reputed to have had several suitors at the time she was "seeing" Grover, including Grover's law partner and mentor, Oscar Folsom. Grover paid child support to the virtually penniless Maria, possibly deciding to accept economic responsibility because, out of all her partners, he was the only bachelor and anyway none of the other men showed much interest in her predicament. He paid for the baby's upkeep until an adoption could be arranged, and even named the child after him and his partner, Oscar Folsom Cleveland. The boy was soon adopted by a couple in western New York and the failing Maria was eventually institutionalised.

It was never proved he was little Oscar's father but no matter, he faced his critics with their sordid revelation and admitted to the affair. He spoke openly about the matter, coming clean with his colleagues, deciding that his honesty should remain constant in the face of Blaine's corrupt wheeling and dealing. A few years earlier a newspaper had made blatant their support for Grover to become Mayor of Buffalo, explaining in print that they supported him for three reasons: "1. He is honest. 2. He is honest. 3. He is honest." But it wasn't an easy road. At Republican rallies his name was greeting with the loud chanting of "Ma, Ma, where's my Pa?" After he was made President, Democratic newspapers turned this jibe around by adding a new line, "Ma, Ma, where's my Pa? Gone to the White House! Ha Ha Ha!"

A friend of Blaine may also have inadvertently contributed to Grover's entrance to the White House. It is thought that the massive amount of Democrat votes from New York City was down to Reverend Samuel D Burchard loudly referring to the Democrat Party as being made up of "rum, Romanism, and rebellion", thereby managing to insult, in one sentence, Irish Americans, Roman Catholics and Southerners and instantly losing his friend the city's important Irish vote – a fatal error for any would-be president.

And so Grover was inaugurated, on 4 March 1885, and immediately went to work, displaying his trademark independence in the presidential role by utterly disregarding trivial niceties that might have been expected of him. For instance, he more than doubled the number of government jobs that came under the Civil Service Commission and he also decided that these desirable positions were to be given to people qualified to perform them as opposed, as was the usual practice, to loyal supporters and friends of the Democrat Party.

The following year Grover made White House history, not so much by getting married but by having his wedding take place in the Blue Room in the White House itself. Naturally there was a bit of gossip attached to the proceedings. He was 49 years old while she was just 21, the youngest First Lady in the history of the United States; but that wasn't what attracted the gossip mongers. She was Frances Clara Folsom, the youngest child of Oscar Folsom, Grover's law partner. Oscar had previously appointed his friend as the executor of the Folsom estate and had also involved Grover in the upbringing of the Folsom children. These two factors proved to be a sticking point for Grover's detractors. The marriage produced four children: Ruth (1891–1904), Esther (1893–1980), Marion (1895–1977), Richard (1897–1974) and Francis (1903–1995).

Grover was President for the next three years. During what would become his first term he supported two major pieces of legislation. Firstly he tried, under the Dawes Act of 1887, to inspire Native Americans to think of themselves as individuals. Tribal lands were surveyed and divided up into allotments to be given to individual Native American families but this backfired after acres and acres of land fell into white hands. In 1885 he ordered a military campaign against the South-western Apache tribe led by Chief Geronimo.

The infamous Geronimo was filled with hatred for white settlers after an attack by Mexican forces left his mother, wife and three children dead in 1851. Always outnumbered, Geronimo and his followers frequently fought against Mexican and United States troops and he urged all the different Indian tribes to do the same. He became famous for his courage and miraculously evaded capture for almost thirty years, until 1886 when he surrendered to General Nelson A Miles at Skelton Canyon, Arizona. His tribe was one of the last important groups of Indian warriors to refuse to accept the United States government.

The second major bill passed under Grover was the Interstate Commerce Act of 1887, which deemed that charges on railroads must be "reasonable and just". The President incurred the wrath of railroad investors by ordering an investigation into the thousands upon thousands of acres of land that they held by government grant, with vague promises of extending train tracks through them for the inhabitants. Over 81,000,000 acres of this land were forfeited and declared to be public domain by the Department of the Interior in recognition of the fact that the promised railroads had never materialised. It was a hugely brave undertaking and, as can be imagined, made the President some very wealthy enemies.

In 1888 Grover and his family packed their bags to leave the White House after failing to win that year's presidential campaign. It is widely believed that he lost out due to fraudulent behaviour on the part of his successor Benjamin Harrison's staff, as he had come top in the popular vote. As they left the mansion the now former First Lady reassured the staff that they would be back in four years' time. And they were.

Portglenone Forest

Grover Cleveland was elected again in 1892, making him the only President in the history of the United States to leave the White House and return for a second term four years later.

He was to be sorely tested during this second term, especially in relation to the Pullman strike of 1894 in Chicago. When the employees of the Pullman Palace Car Company went on strike they were soon joined by the employees of the American Railway Union. Grover took the risky step of employing the army to break the strike, explaining that the strikers were interfering with the US mail. He obtained an injunction in federal court and only when the strikers refused to obey it did he send in the troops, vowing; "If it takes the entire army and navy of the United States to deliver a postcard to Chicago, that card will be delivered."

Sometime in 1893, the President's doctor, Dr RM O'Reilly found a sore, approximately 24mm in length, on the surface of Grover's hard palate. It was later found to be a malignant cancer and surgery was necessary. Because of the timing – the country was experiencing a severe financial depression – Grover decided that his condition was to be kept secret to avoid more panic on the stock market and promptly announced he was taking a cruise for a few days holiday which, considering the timing, invited yet more criticism.

His operation was performed aboard a yacht, the "Oneida", as it sailed off Long Island, by lead surgeon Dr Joseph Bryant, his assistants Dr John F Erdmann, Dr WW Keen, Dr Ferdinand Hasbrouck (dentist and anaesthesiologist) and Dr Edward Janeway. The surgery was conducted through the President's mouth so as to keep facial scaring to an absolute minimum. However, owing to the size of the tumour and the length of the operation his mouth was left severely disfigured, which in turn affected his speech. A second operation saw him fitted with a hard rubber prosthesis which allowed him to speak properly again and it also helped camouflage the tell-tale signs of the first surgery.

The President's team released a story concerning the necessary hasty removal of two rotting teeth which everyone seemed to believe. One newspaper did publish details of the actual operation but none of the surgeons involved agreed to its claims regarding a cancerous tumour. Much later, in 1917, Dr WW Keen wrote an article about the entire operation, naming the President's condition as verrucous carcinoma, stating that the surgery probably saved his life. If you are interested, the cancerous lump is on display to this day at the Mütter Museum in Philadelphia, Pennysylvania.

Grover left the White House for the last time on 4 March 1897, retiring to his estate, Westland Mansion, in Princeton, New Jersey. Some of his loyal supporters wanted him to run again for president in 1904 but by then he was 67 and his health was starting to flag once again. Instead, in 1904, he wrote a book, *Presidential Problems*, explaining and defending his various tactics in office.

Four years later he died from a heart attack, with Frances by his side, and was buried in the Princeton Cemetery of the Nassau Presbyterian Church.

Ian Cochrane

Ian Cochrane was a novelist and creative writing teacher. He was born in Ballymena on 7 November 1941, and later spoke about sharing a bedroom with his parents, three brothers and one sister. There were many hungry, poor days throughout the decade which, ironically, provided Cochrane with rich pickings for his future writings. He attended a small two-roomed country school where he came into contact with teacher/author R.L. Russell, who appreciated the potential in his young pupil and encouraged him to write and dream big about his future. He also encouraged him to read as widely as possible and Cochrane developed a fondness for the American authors, William Faulkner and Flannery O'Connor.

In the late 1950s Cochrane moved to London and after a while managed to earn a full-time wage from his stories. His work was published in a wide variety of literary magazines and anthologies, including 1972's *Penguin Modern Stories*. In 1973 his first novel, *A Streak of Madness*, was published by Allen Lane and hailed as "the creation of an extraordinary gifted artist". However, it would be his second book, *Gone in the Head*, published the following year, that would achieve critical acclaim; it was also a runner-up for the Guardian Fiction Prize.

He had a distinctive voice and his novels are enjoyable for their humour, satire and honesty. His characters are often those on the margins of respectable society: frustrated youths, the unemployed and the temporarily insane. He documents their frequent clashes with the law, religion, and bosses and officials, stripping away the layers of supposed respectability to reveal the inner flaws of society's guardians.

Cochrane was ambiguous about whether a person could really learn to write, despite the fact he taught creative writing for years and was working on a book on the subject. He admitted that he had found that the people who excelled were generally the ones who said in class, "Yeah, I knew that." However, he firmly believed that where there was talent it should be recognised and nurtured; he never forgot the help and encouragement he received from his old school master. His own ability to write he recognised as being a gift, and commented that he couldn't type fast enough to keep up with the flow of words in his mind.

Cochrane had little time for organised religion and in his later years he became interested in Buddhism. He was a man unafraid to do the right thing, even if it meant endangering himself. This was proved one night in 1987 when he spotted two men in an Oxford Street tube station being badly beaten by at least eight others. Cochrane couldn't look the other way, as everyone else was doing, but jumped in to help the stricken two. Inevitably, he was ferociously

Traditional cottages in Kells

punished for his brave intervention, receiving lasting injuries that affected his ability to write. However, he refused to give up and continued to write despite growing ill health. He died at sixty-two years of age from a heart attack on 7 September 2004. An obituary by Maurice Leitch was published in *The Guardian* on Thursday, 23 September that year.

Unfortunately for us not one of his six critically acclaimed novels remains in print today.

Joe Craig

Joe Craig, aka the "Wizard" and the "Prince of Ulster", was born in Gloonan, Ahogill on 11 January 1898 to farmer Joseph and wife, Agnes. On completing his education at Gracehill National School he went to Ballymena to serve his time at Mr Samuel Ruddell's garage in the High Street. Then, in 1925, he joined the official racing team of the Norton Motor Cycle Company.

He was well known locally for passion and success in motor-cycle racing. By 1925 he had won a variety of competitions, including:

> 1st Prize: 4 May 1921; Ballymena and District Motor Club hill climb at Roguery.
> 1st Prize: September 1921; Ballymena and District Motor Club petrol consumption test.
> 1st Prize: 28 September 1921; Ballymena and District Motor Club hill climb at the Collon.
> 2nd Prize: October 1921; South Derry Club's hill climb at Desertmartin.
> 1st Prize: 17 April 1922; Belfast and District Motor Club's hill climb at Red Brae.
> 1st Prize: 8 August 1922; Coleraine and District Club.
> 1st Prize: 20 August 1922; South Derry's Club hill climb.

1st Prize: 28 August 1922; Ballymena and District's Club
hill climb at Roguery.

He was also presented with, in both 1921 and 1922, the Caruth
Challenge for the best all-round performance of a club member.

The year 1923 was probably one of the more important years in
Craig's career in that it brought his first real race, the Ulster Grand
Prix. He must have been a popular mechanic at the garage in High
Street since it was one of his customers who lent him a brand new
Model 18 Norton bike to compete in the race. Craig had an
understanding of the machines as well as a love for the sport. He
decided to use his own bike, a 1921 A.B.C., to make the practice
laps, reserving the Norton's strength for the actual competition. His
primary aim was to complete the route, all 205 miles of it, and to
accomplish this he understood it was imperative to look after the
Norton, using it to perform just two practice laps just to ensure that
everything was working fine. Afterwards he had admitted that his
motto, that day, was simply "I must finish".

Punctures were much more frequent in those days and to counter
any during the race Craig poured some of Jackson's Impervo into
each tyre.

His prudence paid off. Not only did he come first in his race, the
600cc, at 62.99 miles per hour, but his time of three hours, 15
minutes and 17 seconds was declared fastest of the day.

As it turned out, Craig's last race, six years later, in 1929, was also
the Ulster Grand Prix. His bike this time was a 350cc which
unfortunately broke down but not before it ran the fastest lap in Craig's
class at 78.34 miles per hour, thereby setting a new record. Three years
earlier Craig had joined the experimental department of Norton
Motors where he was free to indulge his search for a more reliable
machine and, even better, get paid for doing something he loved. In
1927 one of Craig's colleagues, Walter Moore, designed Norton's first

overhead camshaft engine. Then, in 1930, Arthur Carroll greatly improved the overall design of the Norton racing bike. Also in 1930, Joe Craig succeeded Walter Moore as Development Manager and was largely responsible for the 500cc bike that won the Grand Prix de Europe at Barcelona, which was raced by Tim Hunt.

This was merely the beginning in this stage of Craig's career; he went on to become a huge force in European motorcycle racing as a tuner, development engineer and team boss.

In 1945 Craig was the recipient of a different kind of award when the Institution of Automobile Engineers bestowed the Crompton Medal upon him for his thesis entitled "Progress in Motor Cycle Engines With Some Notes on Combustion".

There was huge excitement for Norton and Craig in 1950 when the first "Featherbed" Norton was produced. The bike had a progressive new frame and suspension and a massively successful debut when four of the new machines beat George Meier's 1939 Senior race record. Craig continued to make leaps and bounds with the single-cylinder engine long after others believed it had done all it could do. In fact he was criticised for his unflagging loyalty to the engine in the 1950s and called "conservative". The Norton bike was being squeezed out of popularity by the Italian Gilera and MV Augusta. However, there was one more glory run in 1955 when three of his single-cylinder engines, raced by Hartle, Surtees and Brett, scored a non-championship Swedish Grand Prix. It was a good time for Craig to step down from his Norton duties and he resigned from his position a few months later.

He married his second wife, Mrs Nellie van Wijngaarden of Rotterdam and moved to Holland to live in semi-retirement. Tragedy struck during a holiday just two years later when the Craigs skidded into another vehicle on an icy motorway in Austria. Joe died at the scene when his heart was pierced by a broken rib. His wife survived the crash with minor injuries.

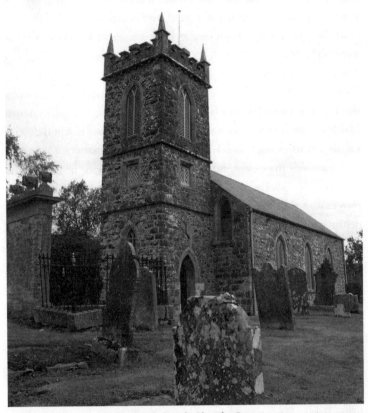

St Saviour's Parish Church, Connor

He might be gone but he is certainly not forgotten, thanks to the TT's Joe Craig Trophy that is presented once a year to the best all-round performance by a British rider. Also, in 1994, Ballymena Borough Council marked the house he was born in, in Ahoghill, with a plaque to commemorate the man and the fantastic contribution he made both to the sport and the machine that is the motorcycle.

Note
James Lansdowne Norton began building motorcycles with French and Swiss engines way back in 1901. Six years later he won the twin-cylinder class in the first TT race. In 1924, a year before his untimely death at 56 years of age, he witnessed his bikes win the Senior and sidecar TTs. The bike wasn't only popular among racing enthusiasts, it was also a favourite with the ordinary rider who appreciated its reliability thanks to the single-cylinder engine with separate gearbox.

One famous rider was Ernest "Che" Guevara who rode a 1939 Norton 500 miles across South America with his friend Alberto Granado, as depicted in the 2004 film, *The Motorcycle Diaries*. Unfortunately the bike didn't live to tell the tale, having collapsed somewhere along the road, but its two riders certainly did.

Steven Davis
Steven Davis, the international footballer, was born in Ballymena on 1 January 1985. He attended Ballymena Academy from 1996 to 2001 before leaving to focus on his football career. Three years later, on 18 September 2004, he made his first appearance for Aston Villa, replacing Nolberto Solana after fifty-seven minutes in a match against Norwich City.

He made his international debut the following year, on 9 February 2005, against Canada. By October he was a regular for both his club and country, missing only one Villa game in 2005/06. He was named Villa's Young Player of the Year, the Fans' Player of the Year, and Player of the Year for that season. A delighted Northern Ireland manager, Lawrie Sanchez, likened him to Frank Lampard.

He assisted in Northern Ireland's famous 1-0 victory over England in a World Cup qualifying match on 7 September 2005. On 21 May 2006, at twenty-one years of age, he became Northern Ireland's youngest (modern day) captain when he assumed the mantle in a match against Uruguay in the USA; unfortunately the team lost that day 1-0. Davis was also part of the team that beat Spain, 3-2, at Windsor Park in September 2006. Less than a year later, on 5 July 2007, Steven left Aston Villa to play at Fulham for a fee of around £4 million.

Timothy Eaton

Timothy Eaton was born in Ballymena in 1834 to a family of Protestant Scottish descent. When he was twenty years old he sailed along with other family members to southern Ontario, Canada, in search of better prospects. In 1861 he set up a bakery business with his brothers, Robert and James, in Kirkton, Ontario. It didn't last beyond a few months but it was a valuable learning experience for the apprentice shopkeeper. Undeterred by failure he simply tried something else, setting up a dry goods store in St. Mary's, Ontario, while notifying his customers that he was switching from bread to dry goods, boots, shoes and medicines which would be sold "cheap and for cash". He devoted almost every waking hour to the shop, boasting that he refused to close while there was anyone anywhere on the street outside.

In 1869 he decided to leave St. Mary's and moved his family to Toronto where he spent $6,500 on procuring Britannia House, the Yonge Street dry goods and haberdashery business. It was another hard slog as he had to compete with as many as twelve other dry goods stores in the surrounding area. But he did it, and was soon in need of several staff. His lasting success was down to his retail initiatives; he did away with haggling (all his goods had one price and one price only), and credit (goods had to be paid for up front before customers left the store). Another innovation was that any purchases made in his shop came with a money back guarantee: "Goods satisfactory or Money Refunded" became the store slogan.

Eaton also introduced the use of electric lights and a sprinkler system into his store which proved extremely beneficial when his neighbour Robert Simpson's shop burnt to the ground while Eaton's was barely touched. In 1884 he introduced his first mail-order catalogue. At thirty-two pages this little miracle provided access to previously hard-to-get-at potential customers in the distant small towns and rural villages, selling clothes, furniture, kitchen utensils, milking machines and other farming equipment.

He appreciated the value of advertising, telling his staff that "If you humbug, do it right." Ads were penned describing his store as "one of the best sights in the city where goods are all marked in plain figures and sold at one price to rich and poor alike". Not surprisingly he was hugely unpopular among the smaller businesses who struggled to compete with him. There were plenty of rallies protesting against the threat of department stores and their like, but to no avail: they were here to stay. In 1905 Eaton opened a second, five-storey store in Winnipeg.

When Timothy died two years later – on 31 January – from pneumonia, his son, John Craig, succeeded him as president of the company. Over the following decades the business continued to flourish, so much so that during the Second World War the Eaton Empire employed a massive 70,000 people, with stores all over Canada.

The new president was the complete opposite of his reserved father. John Craig was a bit of playboy who worked hard and played hard. He wasn't afraid to spend money and splashed out on cars,

Old Church, Cullybackey

racehorses, exotic holidays, as well as building a fifty room mansion to house his family. However, he wasn't a bad man. When, in 1919, he was knighted by George V for his war efforts he celebrated by instigating the five-and-a-half-day week for his then 18,000 employees. Not only that but, during the summer months of July and August, the staff were permitted to take the whole of Saturday off. John refused to take credit for these innovations, explaining that he was just carrying out his father's wishes. After his premature death in 1922, John's wife found herself lambasted by critics when she insisted on delivering high-handed opinions on worldly matters. She regarded the Women's Suffrage Movement as being nothing more than a nuisance because, amongst other things, "it is not restricted to intelligent women". She remained vice-president of the company until her son, John David, became president. Lady Eaton outlived her husband by decades, only dying in 1970 at the grand old age of ninety-one.

Ballymena-born Timothy Eaton is buried in Toronto's Mount Pleasant Cemetery, in the family mausoleum. A stern, quiet and devout Methodist he may have been but when he died several thousand mourners followed his hearse to the cemetery. In 1919 two life-sized statues of Timothy were donated by the Eaton employees to the founding stores in Toronto and Winnipeg to celebrate the company's fiftieth anniversary. Eaton customers established a tradition of rubbing the toes of each statue for good luck. The Toronto statue can now be found in the Royal Ontario Museum, while the Winnipeg statue sits in the MTS Centre, a new arena built on the site that used to house the Eaton shop. Passing hockey fans continue to rub its toe for luck.

Graham Forsythe
The artist Graham Forsythe was born in Ballymena in 1952. His eyesight was so poor from birth that he was classified as legally blind.

When he was six years old his family immigrated to Canada. There wasn't much money which meant that Graham started working when he was just ten, on a potato farm outside Toronto. He was an affable lad and by the time he was twelve his career prospects had much improved; he was now a caddy at the exclusive Hunts Club of Toronto. This is not to say, however, that his studies were neglected. He worked his way through college and graduated, in 1974, from the University of Guelph in Ontario with a degree in Political Science.

He was now twenty-two years of age and had spent more than half of his life working hard; it was time, he felt, to do something else. He decided that he wanted to see as much of the rest of the world as he physically could, starting with America. In 1975 he travelled to New Zealand and found work on a sheep and mixed crop farm. Two years later he flew to Australia and worked at various odd jobs, including a one year stint at timber cruising in the Queen Charlotte Islands. After three years down under, Graham decided that he would like to see Ireland, and spent a year in Killybegs, County Donegal, working as a fisherman. He then returned to Canada and got a job on a commercial salmon trawler off the west coast.

By 1981 Forsythe had tired of working for other people and decided to set up his own business paving roads. There was a lot of work and he was able to employ twelve workers but he still yearned to do something else. He longed to do something creative. His father could pick up any instrument and play it; his sister wrote songs; while his aunt was an Irish dancing champion. He began to write murder mysteries based on the conversations he'd overheard as a child between his father and uncles, who were all policemen working in homicide.

Then, in 1991, his life was changed when he underwent a successful operation to fix his blurry vision. It was a risky operation but the benefit far outweighed any potential problems or complications. And it worked. Suddenly he could see and appreciate clearly the beauty of the world around him – and he began to paint it. He taught himself and refused to categorise his work, saying that "painting can be like meditation... without the prejudices of historical reference or anticipation of its outcome..."

Graham is a member of the Federation of Canadian Artists and has won several Juror Choice Awards. His extremely colourful paintings largely involve still-life, landscapes and luminous abstracts, and are enthusiastically collected.

Eamonn Loughran

The former WBO Welterweight champion was born in Ballymana in 1971.

As an amateur boxer he represented Ireland, taking the silver medal at the 1987 World Junior Boxing Championships in Havana, after beating both America's and Cuba's finest. He turned professional a short while later.

His first professional fight took place, in December 1987, at the Ulster Hall, Belfast, where he beat the Glasweigan boxer Adam Muir on a card that included Dave "Boy" McAuley and Andy Holligan.

In February 1993, he beat Lorenzo Smith to take the WBO title. He defended the title seven times before losing it, in the first round, to the Mexican Jose Luis Lopez in Liverpool, 1996. The shock defeat prompted the Ballymena man to announce his retirement from the sport at the relatively young age of 25 years.

John Lynn, Town Crier

Ballymena used to employ a Mr John Lynn as an official town crier. His job was to address the community, or as many of them as his loud voice could carry to, with only the most local of news. If someone lost something, or maybe a farmer's cow or horse wandered off, Mr Lynn would make the announcement to all and sundry. He lived at the bottom end of Bridge Street and it is said that when he stood on Bridge Street and solemnly rang his large bell for attention,

Glenravel River

his voice could be heard as far as Bryan Street.

His professional stance is described in the book *Ballymena Sketches and Recollections* by a man who remembers him well. After clanging the bell he would keep it in his right hand, while holding the clanger steady with his left, and then he would begin. When he was making a "cry" for an auction, the list of items, usually furniture, would invariably be longer than his memory could sustain and, to cover himself, he would name what he could and finished with the helpful phrase "and other items too numerous to mention". If there was another piece of news, maybe an upcoming event to promote, he would ring the bell again before sounding forth.

Willliam John McBride (MBE)

Now, it is true that William John McBride wasn't born in Ballymena but he did attend Ballymena Academy and joined the Ballymena Rugby Club after he left school. He was actually born in Toomebridge on 6 June 1940 and it would be quite a while before he could think about competitive sports. He only started playing rugby when he was 17 because his father died when he was five which meant he was obliged to pull his weight by helping out on the family farm, before and after his school lessons.

His late start to the sport didn't hinder him in any way; when he was 22 years old he was selected to play for the Ireland national rugby union team. His first match took place on 10 February 1962 against the English national rugby union team at Twickenham. A few months later he was picked to tour South Africa with the British Lions. He continued to play for Ireland throughout the 1960s. He was part of the team that defeated South Africa (the Springboks) in 1965 and was also playing the day they beat Australia on their own turf in Sydney. This fantastic outcome was the first time that a Home Nations team beat a major southern hemisphere team in their own country. McBride was picked again, in 1966, to tour New Zealand

and Australia with the Lions. Two years later he was back in South Africa on yet another tour with the Lions.

In 1971, when he was 31 years old some harsh critics thought of him as being too old to be much use on the field; however he proved them wrong when he helped the Lions to a Test series test win over New Zealand, their first and last series win over the Kiwis. This same year he was awarded an MBE for his services to rugby football.

Three years later he was appointed captain of the 1974 Lions tour to South Africa. The Test series was won 3-0, with one match drawn – the first Lions series ever won in South Africa. By all accounts it was a ferocious battle against the overly aggressive Springboks, with plenty of kicking and punching thanks to the absence of video cameras and sideline officials. Substitutions were only allowed if a doctor verified that a player was physically unable to continue; a swift defence strategy was necessary. It was quickly decided that if, or when, the South African players started to engage wilfully in foul play the Lions were to retaliate fast and hard. A code was established, 99, after the UK emergency number, which signalled for the Lions to attack their nearest rival players.

McBride's international career lasted from 1962 to 1975, during which period he played 17 tests for the Lions and was capped 63 times – 12 of those as captain – by Ireland. He played his last game for Ireland, at Lansdowne Road in 1975. The match was against France and McBride couldn't have chosen a better exit from the game when he scored his first ever Test try for Ireland. His last international match was against Wales on 15 March 1975.

In 2004 he was named in *Rugby World* magazine as "Heineken Rugby Personality of the Century".

Tom McCaughren

Tom McCaughren was born in Ballymena. After his education was completed he began working as a journalist in the *Courier and News* in Dungannon, Country Tyrone. A short while later he began working for the *Ballymena Weekly Telegraph*.

Soon he made the move to Dublin to join the *Irish Times*, writing for this paper for the next thirteen years. It was then that he made the break from print to camera when he became Security Correspondent for RTÉ. It was a tough job which involved covering major crimes throughout the Republic, as well as the early years of the Troubles. He also travelled to troubled areas like the Middle East, Cyprus, Lebanon, Israel, Syria, Bosnia-Herzegovnia, Croatia and Kosovo to report on the activities of the UN Defence Forces.

Amidst all the stresses and unpredictability that went with the territory of his profession, Tom began to form ideas for stories. He already had one book to his name, *The Peacemakers of Niemba*, which he wrote while he was with the *Irish Times*. It was about the bloody ambush by Baluba warriors on an Irish UN patrol in the Congo which resulted in the loss of nine Irishmen who were on a peacemaking mission in the region.

The father of young girls, it occurred to McCaughren that there was little in the way of Irish modern literature for children, and he set about changing that. He wrote five adventure stories for 8 to14 year-olds: *The Legend of the Golden Key*, *The Legend of the Highwayman*, *The Legend of the Corrib King*, *The Silent Sea* and *The Children of the Forge*.

He also wrote three books for teenagers. Two of these were set during the events of 1798: *In Search of Liberty* deals with what happened in his native town of Ballymena during the rebellion, while *Ride a Pale Horse* describes the attack on the house of the High Sheriff of Kildare by rebels led by General Joseph Holt, the last Commander-in-Chief of the United Irishmen. The third novel, *Rainbows of the Moon*, is set on the Irish border during the Troubles and became the key book in a cross-border library project funded by the EU Peace and Reconciliation Programme.

Gracehill Church doorway

McCaughren had another interest in his life – wildlife. Concerned about the welfare of the fox, which was being hunted extensively throughout the countryside for its fur coat, Tom spent two years doing research for what would become a bestselling series of novels with a serious message: *Run with the Wind*, *Run to Earth*, *Run Swift Run Free*, *Run to the Ark*, *Run to the Wild Wood* and *Run for Cover*.

James McHenry

James McHenry was born into a Scots-Irish family in Ballymena in 1753. After a classical education in Dublin he emigrated to Philadelphia at the age of eighteen. He was joined by the rest of his family in 1772. His father and brother set up an import business in Baltimore which James helped out with in between studying medicine under Dr. Benjamin Rush, a well-known doctor in Philadelphia.

During the War for Independence, James served as a military surgeon. In 1776, he was captured by the British at Fort Washington in New York while he was serving with the 5th Pennsylvania Battalion. He was freed less than two years later and returned immediately to duty. In May 1778 he became George Washington's secretary. This change in career helped him make his decision to give up practicing medicine in order to focus on politics and administration. He spent the next two years working for Washington and then, in 1780, he joined the Marquis de Lafayette's staff until he entered the Maryland Senate the following year. The Marquis was a wealthy French aristocrat who had arrived in America to support Washington and the revolution. He refused any payment for his services as a general and diplomat, and on his return to France, he became a key figure in the early stages of the French Revolution.

James McHenry also worked in the Continental Congress, 1783-1786, the first national government of the United States. In 1784 he married Margaret Allison Caldwell.

He didn't make a huge impact at the Philadelphia Convention; in fact he missed a lot of the meetings because of his brother's illness. When he could make it he didn't have too much to contribute to the debates at hand. However, he is partly remembered today thanks to the private journal he kept, an immediate insight into the proceedings. McHenry was tireless in his campaigning for the Constitution in Maryland and attended the state ratifying convention.

In 1787 the man from Ballymena became one of the New World's Founding Fathers when, along with other delegates, he added his signature to the newly penned American Constitution, the supreme law of the United States of America. It was adopted in its original form on 17 September 1787 by the Constitutional Convention in Philadelphia, Pennsylvania, and later ratified by conventions in each state, in the name of "the people". It is possibly the oldest written national constitution and can be viewed at the National Archives in Washington D.C.

Most of the signatories were from the thirteen colonies, while only eight were from elsewhere. McHenry was one of four Irishmen who signed it; two others were English, one was Scottish, and one was from the West Indies.

From 1789 to 1791, McHenry sat in the State Assembly, before returning to sit in the Senate again from 1791 to 1796. George Washington offered him the post of Secretary of War which he, a loyal Federalist, gratefully accepted.

The Federalists wanted a strong central government formed by the country's well-educated elite and they held to the firm belief that those "who own the country ought to govern it". They were led by Alexander Hamilton, while their hero was George Washington, who supported the party but never joined it.

McHenry held on to his Secretary of War post when John Adams succeeded Washington as President but this didn't sit too well with Adams, who constantly found fault with McHenry's work and remained suspicious about his political leanings. In 1800 he forced the Ballymena man to resign, and was immediately accused of maladministration by the Democratic-Republicans. The President was vindicated by a congressional committee.

McHenry took this opportunity for a quieter life and returned to his estate near Baltimore to semi-retire from the pressures of political life at forty-seven years of age. He remained a loyal Federalist and opposed the war in 1812 between America and the British. Britain was warring with France and imposed restrictions on American trade with their enemy. For the United States this was the last straw and they declared war on 18 June. Apart from their trading frustrations the Americans were most upset over British military support for Native Americans who were fighting to retain their territory from white settlers. The war lasted for three years, with a loss of 1,600 British and 2,260 American troops.

Like most of his fellow Founding Fathers, James was a committed Christian and a letter survives which he wrote in 1813 as President of Baltimore's first Bible Society. In it he writes, "Bibles are strong entrenchments. Where they abound, men cannot pursue wicked courses..." Three years later he was dead, at sixty-two years of age, and his remains were buried in Baltimore's Westminster Presbyterian Cemetery. He was survived by two of his three children.

David McWilliams

Singer/songwriter David McWilliams was actually born in the Cregagh area of Belfast on 4 July 1945. However, when he was just three years old, his parents, Sam and Molly, moved to Greenview in Ballymena. There David attended the Model School. He also attended the local technical college before taking an apprenticeship at an engineering works that manufactured torpedoes. But David had much bigger dreams. Music was his first love, though maybe football was a very close second.

Broughshane

He learned to play the guitar as a teenager, motivated by the music of Sam Cooke and Buddy Holly. When he began to write his own songs friends encouraged him to record a demo. In 1966 he walked into Peter's Lloyd's recording studio in Belfast and asked the engineer on duty if he could record some songs he had written. It just so happened that local impresario, Mervyn Solomons, was present and something about the young musician made him delay his next appointment in order to hear him and his material. He recognised McWilliams' potential almost immediately, contacting his brother Phil in London and having him sign the young musician to his new record label, Major Minor Records.

In fact McWilliams had released a début single a few months previously, "God and Country", which failed to attract much attention. By January 1968 he had written and recorded three highly creative albums and was trying to deal with his extraordinarily sudden explosion into the spotlight. It was a massive achievement, especially when you consider the number of years that goes into the making of most chart-topping albums today. The albums were *David Williams Sings David Williams*, *David McWilliams Vol 2* and *David McWilliams Vol 3*. Mike Leander, a producer/arranger who had worked with the likes of Marianne Faithful and the Rolling Stones, kept the arrangements and orchestration as simple as possible to compliment David's subtle style while McWillliams backed himself on six and 12 string guitars.

McWilliams proved hugely popular in mainland Europe, topping the charts in France, Holland and Italy. There was even a restaurant chain in Holland named after his song "Candlelight". Even better than that, the legendary David Bowie admitted to being a fan. At home he toured with the likes of the Dubliners but perhaps the huge success of his first album was never repeated. Daragh O'Halloran, in his book, *Green Beat: The Forgotten Era of Irish Rock*, blames his record company for rushing out the third album so soon after the first two. McWilliams released another three singles with Major Minor Records before the label went bust, to the possible relief of the burnt out musician. His chart successes never made him a rich man. Like many a singer/songwriter before him he lost out on the publishing rights to his music at a possible cost of £2 million.

His most famous, and certainly most covered, song has to be "The Days of Pearly Spencer" which he wrote about a homeless man he had befriended in Ballymena. It actually started life as a B-side to "Harlem Lady". Surprisingly enough it failed to make the British charts on its release in 1967. It would be another 25 years before it would race up the charts to number four, courtesy of Marc Almond of Soft Cell fame in 1992. The song showcased the songwriter's humanity and sincerity and sounds as fresh today as it did on release. The original video which accompanied "Pearly Spencer" on its initial release, featuring a slightly uncomfortable-looking David McWilliams, can still be accessed on the internet, usually alongside comments which show that there is still a vibrant fan base out there for his material.

If McWilliams hadn't made it into the charts he might have had a successful career in soccer. His destiny unfolded only after an injury on the football field took him out of the game for four months, by which time his musical ambitions had been realised. He played for Harryville Amateurs and Rectory Rangers before Linfield Football Club signed him and he immediately became their first-team goalkeeper. Unfortunately – or fortunately, depending on how you look at it – he broke his ankle while playing football with his friends in People's Park. He died on 8 January 2002 aged just 56.

Syd Millar

Dr. Syd Millar CBE was born in Ballymena on 23 May 1934. He played for Ballymena Rugby Football Club and represented Ireland, winning thirty-seven caps as a prop forward, with the ability to play on either side of the scrum. He also played nine times for the British

Lions and coached the triumphant 1974 "Invincibles" on their tour to South America. While his international rugby playing days ended in 1970 he continued to participate in the game until his mid-forties. In 1980, the return tour to South America took place under his management. He went on to assume the role of coach of the Irish team at the 1987 World Cup.

Millar was also a successful businessman, and was awarded an Honorary Doctorate of Science at the University of Ulster in 1992, just before his retirement. In 2004 he was awarded the freedom of Ballymena.

He has been involved with the game for over fifty-five years as player, coach and administrator, and remains a viable force despite two new hips and a triple by-pass. In 2005 he was awarded a CBE in the Queen's Birthday Honours List. He plans to retire from his official duties after the 2007 World Cup.

Colin Murdock

Colin Murdock was born in Ballymena on 2 July 1975. He was capped by Northern Ireland in his youth and there was great excitement about his potential. On leaving school he signed up with Manchester United but a decision to pursue his studies, a law degree, largely prevented him from making a first team appearance over the next five years.

In the summer of 1997 he joined Preston North End and established himself as an extremely clever left-sided defender. Both he and his colleague, Michael Jackson, formed a first-class defence for the Lilywhites and the team was promoted to the English First Division, almost making it to the Premiership. Murdock's ability in the air was particularly notable and he was asked to join the Northern Ireland "B" squad during the 1998/99 season.

In February 2000 he finally made his full international debut for Northern Ireland in a match against Luxembourg, when Sammy

Broughshane

McIlroy substituted him for Mark Williams midway through the second half. The result was a 3-0 victory for Northern Ireland. He won further caps against Hungary and Malta, making an important contribution throughout the 2002 World Cup qualifiers.

Meanwhile he continued to keep his bosses happy at North End with his perfect tackles and dominance in the air. The team won the Second Division Championship in 1999/2000 and David Moyes signed the Ballymena boy up again with a brand new contract.

He scored the team's opening goal of the 2001/02 campaign against Walsall and scored again at the next match. Then he was beset by both injuries and a suspension, which saw him forced to sit out a number of matches. The following year he was sharing the role of central defence with Marlon Broomes after the club reverted to playing with just two centre-halves. Murdock captained the team against Ipswich but then in January 2003 his season was brought to an abrupt end after being injured in the match against Nottingham Forest.

After 212 performances in League and Cup games for North End, Murdock refused to sign a new contract and was placed on the transfer list. He spent one season with Hibernian in Easter Road before joining Crewe towards the end of 2004/05. He was back to fine form and was largely responsible for keeping the team from being relegated. Then, in the summer of 2005, he signed with Rotherham, making 43 league appearances in two seasons and scoring twice.

In the 2004/05 season he scored his first international goal against Austria, in a game which ended in a 3-3 draw.

At the end of the 2006/07 season he left Rotherham and signed a one-year contract with Shrewsbury.

Liam Neeson
On 7 June 1952, William John "Liam" Neeson was born in

Ballymena to Barnard, a caretaker at the local Catholic girl's school, and Katherine Neeson, a cook. He was named Liam after the local priest. His first passion in life was boxing, a sport he took up at the tender age of nine when he first stepped through the doors of the hallowed All Saints club. Two years later he agreed to be in a school play, only because the girl he had his eye on was part of the cast.

By the time he was sixteen he had been Youth Heavyweight Champion of Ireland for three years. Who knows how far he would gone in his beloved sport had he not been hampered by blackouts, which forced him to hang up his gloves. Meanwhile the teacher who had first persuaded Neeson on to the stage set up a local amateur drama company called the Slemish Players. Liam joined the group and took an important role in Brian Friel's *Philadelphia, Here I Come*, winning Best Actor at the Larne Drama Festival. At nineteen years of age Liam moved to Belfast to study mathematics, computer science and geology at Queen's University. However his heart wasn't in it and he stayed for just two terms before returning home to Ballymena. There he worked at a variety of odd jobs from fork-lift operator to driving a truck. He then decided to study at Newcastle's teacher-training college but returned again to Ballymena two years later.

In 1973 he got his first film role, playing Jesus Christ, no less, in the film *Pilgrim's Progress*. He continued to supporting himself with a "day job" in an architect's office and it was his colleagues there who encouraged him to apply to audition for the Lyric Players' Theatre in Belfast. Two years later he moved to Dublin to join the Abbey Theatre. His hard work finally paid off when, in 1980, he was playing the part of Lennie Small in a production of the American author John Steinbeck's bestselling novel, *Of Mice and Men*. Film-maker John Boorman was in the audience that night and he was impressed enough to offer Liam the role of Sir Gaiwain in his movie, *Excalibur*. This was the break the young actor had been waiting for and he accepted the challenge, packing his bags and moving to

London as soon as he was free to. While working on *Excalibur* he met and fell for actress Helen Mirren, most recently a recipient of the Oscar for Best Actress in *The Queen.*

A few years later, Liam decided to move to Hollywood in order to make himself more accessible to the American film industry. In 1987 he landed a role in *Suspect*, a thriller starring Cher and Dennis Quaid, earning a lot of high praise from the critics. He made a name for himself with Sam Raimi's action thriller *Darkman* before taking a lead role in a 1993 Broadway production of *Anna Christie*, starring alongside British actress Natasha Richardson, daughter of Tony Richardson and Vanessa Redgrave. They fell in love and married in July the following year, producing two sons: Micheál Richard Antonio, born in 1995, and Daniel Jack, born in 1996.

Once again a prominent director saw him on stage and immediately wanted him for a film he was putting together – and not just any director. Steven Spielberg offered him the part of Oskar Schindler in his Holocaust epic, adapted from Thomas Keneally's bestselling, prize-winning book, *Schindler's List.* It was a fantastic opportunity and brought Liam an Academy Award nomination for Best Actor. As it happens, the award that year went to Tom Hanks for his performance in *Philadelphia.* Nevertheless, *Schindler's List* established Neeson throughout the acting world as a name to be reckoned with. A string of huge films roles followed, including *Rob Roy*, *Michael Collins* (written and directed by Neil Jordan), *Les Misérables*, *The Haunting*, *Kinsey*, *Love Actually, Kingdom of Heaven, Batman Begins*, *The Chronicles of Narnia* and, of course, *Star Wars Episode I: Attack of the Clones.*

Ian Paisley
Although Northern Ireland's First Minister, the Reverend Ian Richard Kyle Paisley, wasn't born in Ballymena, he moved there from Armagh when he was two years of age. His father, a Baptist minister,

The Thatch Inn, Broughshane

was invited to take over the 200-strong congregation at Hill Street and the family moved into the relatively large pastor's house beside the church.

The young Ian became a born again Christian at six years of age when he was moved by a children's service given by his mother in Hill Street Church, in which she spoke about the Good Shepherd searching for his lost sheep. When the service finished and the other children had left he told his proud mother that he wanted to be a saved lamb as opposed to being a lost sheep. When the church was being renovated half a century later he asked to have the exact pew that he and his mother knelt on together to give thanks for his epiphany.

Ian and his older brother Harold had a strict religious upbringing which resulted in a mannered childhood with few friends and fewer social engagements. They both attended the Model Primary School but weren't encouraged by their parents to mix with their classmates. When Ian was fourteen years old he attended the Ballymena Technical College with the intention of going to the Greenmount Agricultural College near Antrim. Two years later, in the autumn of 1942, Paisley enrolled in the Barry School of Evangelism in South Wales.

As an effective and popular preacher he established and headed the Free Presbyterian Church of Ulster in 1951, which absolutely opposed the "ecumenising" tendencies of the Presbyterian Church. He also built his own Martyrs Memorial Church on the Ravenhill Road in Belfast. In 1970 he succeeded Terence O'Neill as MP for Bannside and was elected the following year to the British House of Commons for North Antrim. He also set up that same year the Democratic Unionist Party (DUP). Eight years later he was elected to the European Parliament.

In 1996 he was elected to the Northern Ireland Forum and then to the Northern Ireland Assembly two years later, where his party wanted to bring about the demise of the Belfast Agreement, which had grown out of events following the first IRA ceasefire in 1994.

Eleven years later the DUP became Northern Ireland's leading unionist party in the 2007 elections to the new Northern Ireland Assembly, thus securing for Paisley the post of First Minister.

Mary Peters

The athlete Mary Peters was born on 6 July 1939 in Halewood, Lancashire, but moved to Ballymena when she was eleven. She was passionate about sport from an early age. On her sixteenth birthday she was the delighted recipient of two tons of sand, a present from her father, with which she could practice her jumping.

She represented Northern Ireland at every Commonwealth Games between 1958 and 1974. Her success at these games came in the form of two gold medals for the pentathlon, and a silver and gold for the shot put.

Her first major international event as a pentathlete was the 1962 European Championships in Belgrade, when she came in fifth after defending champion, the Russian Galina Bystrova. Then, in 1964, she put on a tremendous show at the Tokyo Olympic Games, finishing fourth in what was the first ever Olympic pentathlon (which, in 1984, became the heptathlon).

Mary was also a phenomenal shot putter and in 1966 she set the British record of 16.31 metres, eventually winning this event in the 1970 Commonwealth Games.

In 1968 she went to Mexico for the Olympics but there was an upset when she injured her ankle and only managed to come in ninth. At this point in her career she was thirty-one years old and probably thought that the Mexico Games were her last chance of Olympic success. In 1970 she won again at the Commonwealth Games in Edinburgh, where she took the gold in both the pentathlon and the shot put. She attained the rank of sixth in the world that year. She also won a scholarship to train in the warmer, and peaceful, climate of California, from where she returned new and improved, in fighting form for the 1972 Olympics at Munich.

She was now 33 years old and determined to make this her best performance. Her two serious rivals were Heide Rosendahl and world record holder, Burglinde Pollack, from East Germany. By the time of the 200m, the last event of the pentathlon, Mary knew that if she finished a mere 1.3 seconds behind Rosendahl she would lose the gold medal. So she ran the race of her life and came in first, to a rapturous applause from Irish and English fans everywhere. On her return she was named the "BBC Sports Personality of the Year".

In 1973 Mary was made an MBE (Member of the Order of British Empire). Seventeen years later she was made a CBE (Commander), and then a DBE (Dame Commander) in 2000. The Mary Peters Track, at the Malone Playing Fields in Belfast, was named in her honour. When she retired from competing Mary took on the role of manager, managing several UK athletic teams at the Olympic Games and at other international competitions. She was also a member and Vice-Chairman of the Northern Ireland Sports Council, and was President of the British Athletics Federation from 1996 to 1998. For her tireless promotion of sport she received, in 2001, the Lifetime Achievement Award at the *Sunday Times* Sportswoman of The Year Awards. Mary is also renowned for her relentless charity work.

Note: The 1972 Olympics will never be forgotten worldwide thanks to the Arab extremists from the Black September organisation who kidnapped 11 Israeli athletes and their officials and then murdered them when confronted with the German police.

Saint Patrick

Hail Glorious Saint Patrick. The patron saint of Ireland was possibly one of the earliest, most famous visitors to the surrounding area of Ballymena, though at the time of his visit he was as far from fame and sainthood as anyone else.

War monument in Memorial Park

He was born in 387AD at Kilpatrick, near Dumbarton, in Scotland to Calphurnius, whose family had originated from Rome, and Conchessa, who was related to St. Martin of Tours, the patron saint of Gaul. Little is known about his childhood but when he was sixteen he was snatched away from the life he knew when Irish marauders invaded his village. The young Patrick was brought back to Ireland where he was sold into slavery to a chieftain called Milchu from Dalriada. For the next six years the boy tended his master's flock in the valley of the Braid River and on the slopes of Slemish.

It proved the perfect preparation for a future missionary. During his six years he nurtured his faith with daily prayer. He also learned how to speak the language fluently, the language he would use to convert the people of Ireland. Furthermore, his master, Milchu, was a druidical high priest which allowed Patrick to study Druidism up close so that when he returned to Ireland to preach Christianity he knew exactly what he was up against. But first he had to remove himself from his present daily grind. God sent an angel to prompt him to change the course of his life. Finally, at the age of twenty-two, Patrick fled his life of slavery, escaping two hundred miles to Westport to board a ship that would bring him back home. In a matter of days he was back among the people he loved although he wouldn't allow himself to bask in their embraces for long. He was now filled with a mission to bring the Word of God to the pagan peoples of Ireland, banishing snakes on the way. He had visions of the Irish children calling for his return: "O holy youth, come back to Erin, and walk once more amongst us."

The summer of 433 is generally believed to be the year of his return visit, twenty-four years after he fled the country as a runaway slave. The first thing that Patrick wanted to do was initiate a meeting with his former master in order to pay his own ransom price which would ensure his legal freedom from slavery. He also wanted to bless Milchu in the hope of inspiring him to mend his cruel ways.

On the way back to Slemish he built up quite a reputation with news of his miracles and his message of love causing quite a stir. He took a boat to Strangford Lough and then determined to walk the rest of the way but first there were obstacles to overcome. A local chieftain, Dichu, attempted to block Patrick from reaching the slopes of his youth. However, when he drew his sword his arm felt as heavy as stone and he was unable to strike the priest. Instead of killing Patrick, Dichu became one of his earliest devotees.

Patrick's intention to meet with Milchu was thwarted. His old master panicked at the idea of being, according to an ancient record, "vanquished by his former slave". In a blind panic he chose to avoid a confrontation by setting fire to his mansion, which was stuffed up with all his riches. As the flames enveloped his home he made one last act of defiance by throwing himself into the fire. Patrick arrived too late to save him.

Slemish has been a popular place of pilgrimage for many centuries now, particularly on 17 March. Long before Saint Patrick ended up herding flocks the mountain was actually an active volcano. Wild flowers, some quite rare, can be found growing on its grassy slopes. It's not an easy climb at 180 metres, with plenty of jagged edges and rocks and boulders, but the view from the top more than makes up for it. On reaching the summit, look north to the ruins of Skerry Church on a hilltop, where Milchu's fort once stood. This was the ancient burying place of the O'Neills at Clandeboye.

Sequah the Healer

Ballymena was one of many towns throughout the island to frequently play host to Sequah, who would have been well-known to the locals at the turn of the twentieth century. The healer was a travelling salesman, a North American Indian, in fact, or at least that was his claim: North American or not, he certainly was a showman who knew his audience.

Weeks before a visit there would be posters all over town to prepare his potential consumers. He always stayed in the same place, the Adair Arms Hotel, which suggests a man who obviously liked his comforts and routine. At that time there was bit of waste ground between the bottom of Bridge Street and Clonovon and it was here he would put on his seductive performance, as that of a healer, with a bottle of pills for every ill possible. He left no stone unturned in presenting his wares to the spellbound audience of locals.

He didn't travel alone, or in much style either: his transport was an "Indian-type" horse-drawn wagon and his companions were a small travelling band who accompanied him on his every visit; they too were dressed like Indians. The short journey from the hotel to the site, where a platform had been especially erected for the band, and back again, after the show, was always a bit of an event in itself. Leaving his lodgings he would climb into the wagon and slowly make his way to the Bridge Street "stage", the band following behind on foot, playing their instruments. The local children would clamour around the wagon as Sequah was known to call a halt to the horses, stand up, reach deep into his pockets, and fling coins to the baying youngsters.

By the time he reached his destination there was already a good-sized crowd waiting for him. The band would take to the platform while Sequah opened the show by greeting his audience. According to a well-seasoned eyewitness he loved describing the sun as "God's Golden Globe"; the rays of the sun were an important ingredient in his medicine. One in particular, the "Prairie Flower", had the ability to cure almost anything.

The walking wounded would then be invited up to the stage to be cured. This is what the people had been waiting for; the crippled and the sick would make their way towards him in large numbers, some hobbling on crutches and walking sticks, others, perhaps were too weak to walk, being carried by relatives. Once they were onstage,

Memorial Park

Sequah would address his audience again to announce how fast he was going to cure these poor afflicted.

One by one the patients were led by the showman behind a screen where they would be "cured". The crippled could now walk and the sick were sick no longer, and they would make their way back triumphantly to their friends with no need of assistance. Or so the story goes.

Hundreds more had their rotten teeth pulled out in front of the crowd in what was described by Sequah as a completely painless operation. However, as eyewitnesses pointed out, any screams of pain would have been drowned out by the band, which was always playing loudly throughout the proceedings.

The healer's visits usually lasted for a fortnight and Saturdays were especially interesting. On these days a race was held in which the only competitors were the townspeople he had cured. It must have been quite a sight as young and old, the formerly crippled and sick, took their marks against one another. After the race Sequah would do a roaring trade on "Prairie Flower", the day's sport being the perfect advertisement for his product.

When he left Ballymena for another town the local chemists stocked up on the medicine and would invariably sell out within a few weeks. Eyewitnesses allude to the smell of the herb which was stronger than the smell of rotten flax. They also mention the fact that once Sequah left there was little permanent trace of his visit; all the people he had "cured" usually reverted back to being sick and crippled again.

Jack White
Jack White was born just outside Ballymena, in the village of Broughshane. His maternal grandfather was chaplain of the Royal Chapel in Windsor Park. After attending Windsor College from 1892 to 1896 his father enrolled him as a King's Cadet at Sandhurst.

In 1899, as a young man, Jack followed his father, an Anglo-Irish landowner, into the British Army and fought against the Boers in South Africa with the 1st Gordon Highlanders, where he proved fearless, and not only in the face of the enemy.

At the battle of Doorknop he was one of the first to go over the top of the trench. When he looked back he spotted a terrified boy of 17 years, paralysed by fear, unable to follow his fellow soldiers. Just then an officer spotted the young "coward" and roared at White to shoot him. Jack immediately trained his gun on this officer and threatened to shoot him instead.

At the end of the war he became his father's aide when he was made Governor of Gibraltar and then, later again, went on to serve with the 2nd Gordons in India. He tendered his resignation to the army in 1905 and returned home where he became quickly involved in the turbulence surrounding the possibility of Home Rule being bestowed on Ireland. Sir Edward Carson was rounding up his anti-Home Rule supporters while the original UVF was threatening to declare war on the British government if the bill was passed.

Jack disagreed with Carson and his desire for a solely Unionist Ulster. He decided to organise a meeting, for Protestants only, in Ballymoney to prove that Carson was not representative of all Ulster's Protestants. The Town Hall, the meeting place, was adorned with Union flags when the speakers, including Sir Roger Casement, took to the stage in front of approximately 500 people.

As a result of this meeting Jack was invited to Dublin where he met James Connolly and was converted to socialism. The year was 1913 and workers in Dublin were striving for union recognition in the face of hard-line, immovable figures like Corkman William Martin Murphy, founder of Independent Newspapers. Jack was much impressed by what he saw and offered his services to the ITGWU (Irish Transport and General Workers' Union) at Liberty Hall. Within a month Jack set up the Citizen Army with its object to "sink all differences of birth, property and creed under the common name of the Irish people". The Army would patrol picket lines to protect the strikers from scabs and the harsher elements of the Dublin Metropolitan Police.

Later on he offered his services to the Volunteers, believing that an efficient and prepared army should convene to stand up to British rule. He travelled to Derry to make himself known to the local brigade of Volunteers but was rebuffed by those who accused him of only wanting to look after Protestant interests.

Following Dublin's 1916 Easter Rising, James Connolly was one of several rebel insurgents sentenced to death. Jack immediately made his way to South Wales where he endeavoured to bring the miners out on strike in a vain effort to save Connolly's life. He wound up behind bars in Pentonville Prison for three months, where he met his old acquaintance, Sir Roger Casement, who was due to hang. Casement had been tried for treason after attempting to smuggle in a shipment of German guns to help with the Rising. The two prisoners had fallen out a couple of years previously and now took the opportunity, presented unintentionally by the British government, to patch up their friendship again before Casement's death on 3 August 1916.

After his release from prison Jack put on his good clothes to have tea with Countess Markievicz on the terrace of the House of Commons.

When Jack came home he found himself to be something of a political misfit. The unionists regarded him as a "Shinner" while the nationalists thought him an Orangeman. After a while he found himself drifting towards the new Communist Party but it was a temporary interest as he had his doubts about them and refrained from actually joining the group. It was also around this time that he worked for a while in London with Sylvia Pankhurst's anti-parliamentary communist group, the Workers Socialist Federation.

Chester Alan Arthur's Cottage

In 1934 a special convention took place in Athlone where the attendants, made up of 200 former IRA volunteers, prominent socialists, communists and trade unionists decided to set up a Republican Congress. The focus was on small farmers and the ordinary worker, and immediately appealed to White, who went about setting up a Dublin branch made up of British ex-servicemen. Thanks to him there was the extraordinary sight of British former squaddies marching behind the Congress banner being cheered by Dubliners for their part in a demonstration against war and poverty.

But it wasn't all sweetness and light. When 200 Belfast Protestants workers arrived to take part in the Republican Wolfe Tone Commemoration that year, the infamous Sean McBride had his IRA men attack them, saying he didn't want any red banners spoiling their Catholic day out in Bodenstown.

The Belfast man carrying the second banner, from the James Connolly Club in Belfast, was John Straney, a milkman from Ballymacarret. He would lose his life five years later at the Battle of the Ebro while fighting the Fascist forces of General Franco.

Perhaps inevitably, trouble flared between the different ambitions of the congress, resulting in a split; one group wanted to focus only on attaining a Workers' Republic while the other group, led by the Communists, believed that the congress should work with Fianna Fáil to reunite the island of Ireland. When most of the first group walked away in frustration from the congress – to end up in the Labour Party – White remained in the considerably depleted organisation.

In April 1936, the remaining members took part in the annual Easter Rising Commemoration and found themselves continually and viciously attacked by Blue Shirt gangs. Jack White was forced to physically defend himself with his blackthorn walking stick and ended up badly injured after being hit on the head with an iron cross.

The Blue Shirts were actually the Army Comrades' Association which was founded in 1932 by army veterans, as a sort of Fascist reaction to Fianna Fáil's election that year. Led by the former Commissioner of the Garda Síochaná, Eoin O'Duffy, they stood for the interests of the large farmers against the smaller arable farmers – the rich versus the poor if you like – and styled themselves on the Continental Fascist with their uniform of blue shirts and the raised arm salute.

When the Spanish Civil War broke out General O'Duffy and 700 of his members went over to the aid of Franco's forces. Meanwhile the Communist Party and prominent republicans formed the Connolly Column to aid the battle against Franco's army. The 57 year old Jack White travelled to Spain as part of a Red Cross ambulance crew to make his contribution and was delighted to see Irish Catholics and Protestants fighting together against the common enemy of Fascism. Alongside his work with the Connolly Column he also trained men in fighting with firearms and gave lessons to village women in how to defend themselves with a gun.

However, he still refrained from committing himself to the Communist Party and grew uneasy over what he perceived as the Irish being increasingly manipulated by the group. Frank Ryan, secretary of the congress, accused Jack of being a "Trotskyite" and a traitor. White promptly resigned from the International Brigade and offered his services to the CNT, the Anarcho Syndicalist Trade Union Confederation. He had come to the conclusion that only the "anarchists" were on the right track and wished to join them.

Anarchism was introduced in Spain in 1868 by Giuseppi Fanelli and was immediately welcomed by both the workers and Spanish peasants as a superior alternative to capitalism and the state. The movement flowed back and forth between the rural and the urban dwellers as union organisers and anarchist militants traipsed out to address the villages while country peasants, in turn, entered cities like Barcelona in their search for a job. As a result of this context, anarchism was forever associated with the labour movement.

Followers appreciated the practice of direct action and solidarity which promoted the idea of educating yourself so as to be able to identify and solve problems. If people were educated then they would know exactly what they wanted, as opposed to clubbing together in an angry mob and making ridiculous demands that couldn't possibly be taken seriously.

Jack White was hugely impressed by their level of organisation and after a few months in Spain had become a fully signed up member, writing the pamphlet, *The Meaning of Anarchism*. He also helped to produce *Freedom*, the anarchist paper which is still published in London today. Furthermore, White also helped organise the meetings at the National Trade Union Club where support for Spanish anarchism was loudly proclaimed. The CNT asked him to go to London to work with the legendary Emma Goldman.

"Red Emma" was a life-long anarchist known for her writing and stirring speeches. Born in Lithuania on 27 June 1869 her fiery, independent spirit prevented her from allowing her father to marry her off when she was just 15 years of age. Two years later she was shipped off to Rochester, New York to live with her half-sister. Life in America for a penniless Jewish immigrant was far from luxurious and Emma spent several aching, sweating years working in a textile factory. In 1887 she married her colleague, Jacob Kershner, which immediately granted her US citizenship.

She became an anarchist after the 1886 Haymarket Riot in Chicago – or, to be more precise, what followed the riot. On 4 May, at about 8.30pm, the McCormick reaper workers were rallying for an eight hour day at the Haymarket, an area between Halsted and Des Plaines Street. Due to a poor turnout they decided to move their rally to Des Plaines Street, north of Randolph Street. Things were fine for a couple of hours but then chaos ensued at 10pm just as the group were finishing up for the night. About 200 workers were immediately confronted by 176 policemen whose Inspector, John Bonfield,

Slemish

ordered them to leave the area and go home. Suddenly a bomb was thrown into the middle of the police who naturally panicked and began to discharge their weapons. Shots were also fired from the workers' side. The bomb killed one policeman outright and six others died later; sixty more were injured and it was later shown that most of the wounded had been shot by their own bullets.

In the tense days that followed all well-known anarchists and socialists were arrested on suspicion of having thrown the bomb. Some very dubious evidence led to the eventual trial of eight anarchists, seven of whom were sentenced to death and four of whom were actually hanged. The presiding judge caused uproar when he told the men that they were not just on trial because of the Haymarket bomb, but because they were anarchists.

The incident proved to be a huge catalyst in Emma's life and she promptly left her husband and sister, heading to New York where she befriended Johann Most, the editor of a German anarchist paper, and began her life anew as a revolutionist complete with several prison sentences.

(In fact the attitude in the Haymarket trial was not a one-off. In 1922 two Italian immigrants, Nicola Sacco and Bartolomeo Vanzetti, were sentenced to death for murders that they had not actually been found guilty of committing. When handing out the sentence the judge confirmed that while they may not have carried out the killings the two men were still enemies of the state because they were anarchists. They were executed by electrocution on 23 August 1927.)

It was many years later, when she was 67 years old, that Emma arrived in Spain to support the Spanish anarchist movement, and she was delighted to witness anarchism as a living reality.

Emma Goldman died from a stroke three years later in Toronto, on 14 May 1940. If you would like to see her today then you could do worse than visit the Chinese restaurant on Spadina Avenue in

Toronto, formerly the union hall where she delivered many a speech, and where her body was displayed after her death. It is said that her ghost resides there as if waiting to be called once more, to address her followers.

When Jack was in London he took Spanish lessons and met his second wife, Noreen Shanahan. Noreen, a Catholic, came from a wealthy Dublin family, her father being a government official. As with his first marriage, which had also been to a middle-class Catholic, his union with Nora was not to last, though it did produce three sons. It is odd that Jack chose two Catholics to share his life with as he held some very negative views regarding Catholicism. In Spain he had applauded the people of Cataluna for not being heavily influenced by Rome or their parish priests; he deplored this tendency in the Irish Catholics to be so easily stirred up from the pulpit.

Jack had inherited the White Hall family home and property on his father's death in 1912, though it only properly passed into his hands on his mother's death in 1935. He finally settled down in Broughshane in 1938 but continued to remain in contact with his political comrades. He often rode into Ballymena on his grey horse to attend the Saturday market.

Seven years later, in the General Election of 1945, he put himself forward as a candidate, the "Republican Socialist" Antrim representative, and held a meeting at the local Orange Hall to present his case. However, his name never made it to the ballot paper. Six months later he was dead from cancer.

He spent his last weeks in a Belfast nursing home and, after a private ceremony, he was buried in Broughshane in the White family plot in the First Presbyterian Church. It is thought that his family destroyed most of his papers and writings after his death, so ashamed were they of his life as a persistent rebel.

Nigel Worthington

Born in Ballymena on 4 November 1961, the 1981 "Young Footballer of the Year" – then the star of Ballymena United – attracted attention from the likes of the Notts County manager, Jimmy Sirrel, who arrived that summer to sign him up for his club.

He spent the next three years establishing himself as a regular at Meadow Lane. Then, in February 1984, he was brought to Hillsborough by Howard Wilkinson to join Sheffield Wednesday in their successful entry to the First Division. A few months later Worthington won his first cap for Northern Ireland in the Home Championships match against Wales. International games followed, including a trip to Mexico for the 1986 World Cup Finals. He proved a consistent and reliable player over the following decade. One memorable occasion was the return of the League Cup to Hillsborough after an absence that stretched all the way back to 1935, thanks to the unforeseen thrashing meted out to favourites, Manchester United, which ended in a colossal 10-0 score.

In the 1993/94 season he was named Northern Ireland's "Player of the Year" and became Sheffield Wednesday's most capped player. After appearing in 417 games for the Owls he made a break in June 1994, rejecting his new contract in favour of joining with old boss Howard Wilkinson again, albeit this time at Leeds United, where he spent the next two years braving the infamous Elland Road boo-boys.

A year at Stoke followed and he was then appointed player-manager of Blackpool. Meanwhile his 66th, and final cap was gained when he came on as a substitute in the 1997 friendly against Belgium which saw Northern Ireland triumphant with 3-0. Shortly afterwards he decided to concentrate on being a manager and, in December 2000, was appointed caretaker manager of Norwich City following the resignation of Bryan Hamilton. He was then given the role on a full-time basis after proving himself more than capable. The 2001/02

Jack White's family grave

season saw him take the Canaries to an exciting First Division play-off final against Birmingham City in Cardiff, which was brutally lost on penalties.

Three years later he headed Norwich's promotion to the Premiership as First Division champions with a club-record total of 96 points. To maintain standards he was forced to sign Premiership players on loan, including Manchester City's Darren Huckerby and Aston Villa's Peter Crouch. That Christmas Norwich beat Ipswich 2-0, going straight to the top of the League. His first season as manager in the Premiership ended badly with Norwich being soundly trumped on the last day by Fulham, 6-0, while West Brom beat Porsmouth. Consequently Norwich ended up in 19th place with a total of 77 goals conceded. Worthington stayed with Norwich for six years, a few of them quite stressful when he had to weather poor results coupled with the sometimes loud opposition of fans to his managerial style.

On 11 April 2007 he was appointed caretaker manager, following Rob Kelly's sacking, of Leicester City for their last five games of the season. His first match was three days later – against Norwich City. He was in the running for the full-time managerial position but the role was given to Martin Allen on 25 May.

Worthington was appointed manager of the Northern Ireland team on 1 June 2007 on a short-term contract that lasts until the end of the Euro 2008 qualifying tournament.

Alexander Wright

Alexander Wright was born in Ballymena in 1826. He became a dedicated and fearless soldier during the Crimean War, as a private in the 77th (East Middlesex) Regiment of Foot (which, in 1881, became the Middlesex Regiment [Duke of Cambridge's Own], British Army).

His courage shone out during a tense battle at Sebastopol on 22 March 1855 in the Crimea when he showed great fortitude in repelling a sortie. A month later, on 19 April, he distinguished himself in the battle to take the Russian Rifle Pits, holding his cool under particularly heavy fire and artillery, as well as taking the time to encourage the men who were fighting alongside him. For these two events, and for all of his acts of bravery which continued throughout the war, he was awarded the Victoria Cross, the most prestigious of awards for British and Commonwealth forces, bestowed for "the most conspicuous bravery, or some daring or pre-eminent act of valour or self-sacrifice, or extreme devotion to duty in the presence of the enemy".

A recommendation for the VC is usually issued by an officer at regimental level and must be supported by three witnesses. The recommendation is passed up through the ranks before being made to the Secretary of State for War, now the Secretary of State for Defence, and then the monarch, whose permission is required.

The award is a cross pattée, 41mm high and 36mm wide, showing a crown surmounted by a lion, with the inscription "For Valour". The inscription was originally to be "For Bravery" but Queen Victoria thought that this might imply that only the recipients of the award were brave. A tiny "V" is the joiner between the actual cross and the bar through which the ribbon is folded. This bar is decorated with laurel leaves and engraved with the recipient's name, rank, number and unit. There is a circle on the back of the medal which is then engraved with the date on which the brave deed or deeds took place. The crimson, or wine-red, ribbon is 38mm wide.

Alexander's cross is on display at the Princess of Wales's Royal Regiment (Queen's and Royal Hampshires) Museum at Dover Castle in England. A total of 169 recipients of the Victoria Cross are Irish-born.

PART THREE
SPORT

Ballymena Road Club

In 1896 James Kyle, an official with Ballymena and Antrim Athletic Club, chaired a meeting which elected a secretary, captain and treasurer for Ballymena's new cycling club. A few weeks later the town had its first cycle run which was held at the Pentagon Lamp. More than 300 locals turned out to watch just twelve cyclists, a sure sign of the magnitude of the event for the town. It was also covered by the local newspaper that referred to the bicycles in equestrian terms, the riders "turned the horses' heads" in the direction of Broughshane and so forth. There was also mention of a few riders/cyclists coming off their machines at a dodgy part of the road, but no one was hurt.

Ballymena was a popular spot for races at this time because it was the only place in Ireland with a hard track, now the location of the showgrounds. Harry Reynolds, the only Irish world cycling champion, raced there in the early 1900s. It is possible that one of the prizes on offer was the Road Club's "Red Hand Trophy", which dates back to 1898.

We move forward now to 1954 with the formation of the present Ballymena Road Club by cyclists from the only other club around, the Old Bleach in Randalstown. Six Old Bleach members, from Ballymena, decided to start up a club for their hometown: Carson Conway, Sammy Kerry, Joe McAuley, Stan Finlay, Fred Swan and Smyth Wallace. The first proper meeting took place on 4 October 1954 behind Saunders' Chemist in Bridge Street. Twenty-six enthusiasts turned up to elect a president, Sam McQuigg; chairman,

Matt Eaton; secretary, Stan Finlay; race secretary, Jim Trimble; and treasurer, Seamus Blaney. The following year the season opened with the first ten miles trial for the Frank Gardiner Cup.

In 1956 there was jubilation when the club, as represented by Sammy Kerr, Joe Caldwell and Fred Wylie, won the Andrews Cup 100 mile time trial. Kerr also won second prize in the Northern Ireland 100 Miles Championship, while the Kerr-Caldwell-Wylie trio scored again by winning the team medal in this competition.

Kerr could do no wrong. He was Ireland's best finisher in the 1958 Tour of the North, and with Sammy Connor and Alan Mark, he won the Sun Cycles Shield in the Chemco Cup Classic, a 25-mile time trial which was held in Dublin. Not surprisingly Kerr was selected to represent Northern Ireland in the 1958 Commonwealth Games in Cardiff. He gained many international honours as well as winning, on no fewer than four occasions, the title of Northern Ireland Best All Rounder.

The Sixties possibly belonged to the Caldwell brothers. Gordon won the All Ireland Road Race in 1964 while Wallace rode the 1,300 miles that was the Tour of Britain four years earlier. Wallace's potential was cut short when he was killed in 1968 during a race at Burrow-in-Furness.

Billy Kerr enjoyed constant success during the late Seventies and early Eighties. He won the Tour of the North two years running in 1978 and 1979. He also won the 1979 Sealink International Stage Race in England. He won the *Ras Tailteann*, the Tour of Ireland, the Northern Ireland, and the All Ireland Race championships. In one terrific season he won all six time trial championships, 25, 50 and 100 miles, Northern Ireland and All Ireland.

Apart from the many successes the Ballymena Road Club has enjoyed, the club is also renowned for the huge amount of money its diligent members have raised for the likes of Multiple Sclerosis and the Ulster Cancer Foundation.

THIS MONUMENT IS ERECTED TO PRESERVE THE MEMORY OF THE REVᴰ FULKE WHITE, OF WHITE HALL, WHO WAS MINISTER OF BRAID, FOR 29 YEARS, AND WHO DIED THE 24ᵀᴴ AUGUST 1710. ALSO OF HIS SON JAMES, WHO SUCCEEDED HIM AS MINISTER OF BRAID, AND WHO DIED THE 24ᵀᴴ AUGUST 1761.

ALSO OF HIS GRANDSON JOHN WHITE, ESQ. WHO DIED SEPTEMBER 1770.

ALSO OF HIS GREAT GRANDSON JAMES WHITE, ESQ. WHO DIED JULY 1804.

LIKEWISE JANE, WIFE OF THE LATTER WHO DIED JANᵂ. 1804.

ALSO JANE, HIS DAUGHTER WHO DIED SEPTᴿ 1825.

ALSO VICTORIA, HIS DAUGHTER WHO DIED JUNE 1837.

ALSO OF JOHN WHITE, ESQ. HIS SON WHO DIED 18ᵀᴴ FEBRUARY 1857, AGED 71 YEARS.

ALSO OF HIS GRANDSON JAMES WHITE, WHO DIED MARCH 16ᵀᴴ 1860, AGED 27 YEARS.

ALSO OF FRANCES, WIFE OF JAMES ROBERT WHITE, ESQ. OF WHITE HALL, WHO DIED 7ᵀᴴ JANUARY 1870, AGED 69 YEARS.

JAMES ROBERT WHITE, ESQ. DIED THE 9ᵀᴴ JANUARY 1872, AGED 85 YEARS.

JOHN WHITE, ESQ. C.B. 3ᴿᴰ SON OF THE ABOVE NAMED JAMES ROBERT WHITE, FORMERLY FELLOW OF QUEENS COLLEGE OXFORD, AND PRINCIPAL ASSISTANT SECRETARY TO THE BOARD OF EDUCATION LONDON, DIED 12ᵀᴴ JANUARY 1912, AGED 76 YEARS.

GEORGE STUART WHITE, FIELD MARSHAL, V.C., G.C.B., G.M.G.S.I., G.C.M.G., G.C.I.E., G.C.V.O., J.P., D.L., Co. ANTRIM, SECOND SON OF THE ABOVE NAMED JAMES ROBERT WHITE, DIED 24ᵀᴴ OF JUNE 1912, AGED 76 YEARS.

CAPTAIN JAMES ROBERT WHITE, D.S.O. SON OF THE ABOVE BORN MAY 28ᵀᴴ 1879, DIED FEB 3ᴿᴰ 1946.

Headstone to the White family grave

Ballymena United (The "Sky Blues")

This football club was set up in 1928 and it was in August of that year that the club had its first ever Irish League game. They played the favourites at the time, Belfast Celtic, at the Showgrounds on 20 August, unfortunately losing 3-0. Within five days, however, the young team scored its first points, while a few weeks later they garnered their first win. They finished sixth in the league, while their Irish Cup efforts proved much more successful: they beat Glentoran, Broadway United, Coleraine and Belfast Celtic, and took the title. Unfortunately they failed in their defence of it against Linfeld the following year, though they didn't part with it easily after a tight 4-3 result.

Their luck worsened in the 1930s when the club was besieged with money problems as well as poor playing. In particular the year 1935 was not a good one; the team was obliged to withdraw from the league and went into liquidation. However, all was not lost as the club reformed again with its old players. It wasn't an easy road and there was great excitement when the team made the Irish Cup Final, only to lose – again – to Linfeld. Then, in 1940, they reached another cup final, this time proving triumphant by beating Lurgan 2-0. The Cup was back in Ballymena after eleven years.

A break from football was enforced when the club gave up their grounds to the military as part of the war effort. It was 1946 before they returned to the league. Success was once again theirs when they beat Linfield 2-0 in the County Antrim Shield Final. Up to then, this trophy had never been outside of Belfast, having spent its time divided between Cliftonville, Distillery, Linfeld and Glentoran. It must have enjoyed its stay in Ballymena because it came back in 1951 after a 2-0 victory over former hosts Cliftonville.

After Belfast Celtic left the Irish League in 1949 Ballymena plucked the best players for its club, including Billy McMillan, who assumed the role of player-manager at the club. McMillan was later replaced by Walter Rickett and the club reached another Irish Cup Final in 1951, losing to Glentoran 3-1. Another win was due, this time over Crusaders (3-0) at the Festival of Britain Cup. Unfortunately, bad times were just around the corner once more; fortunately the good folk of Ballymena could be depended on when, in 1955, the club launched a public appeal for financial help. Debts were cleared and it was time to think about football again.

In 1958, under the management of Scot Alex McCrae, the team won the Irish Cup, beating long-time opponents Linfield 2-0. They made it to another final, in 1959, of the Showpiece Cup and were favourites against Glentoran. It was a tense match that ended in a 1-1 draw; when the match was replayed, the Ballymena men lost in a shocking 2-0 result. Revenge was sweet in 1960, under new manager Geoff Twentyman, when Ballymena beat Glentoran 3-1 to take the Ulster Cup.

There followed a line of unsuccessful managers after Twentyman's luck soured: George Smyth, Dave Hickson, Alex Parker, and Dave Hickson for a second turn. Alex McCrae was brought back, helping the team to the 1970 Irish Cup Final at Solitude, only to see them fall against Linfield 2-1.

McCrae later resigned after a board member complained about his wages. He was replaced by Arthur Stewart as player-manager. In 1971 the team took the City Cup after playing Ards at the Oval, but Ards made up for their loss three years later when they beat Ballymena in the Irish Cup Final 2-1. Meanwhile Ballymena won the Gold Cup, with Glentoran losing 3-2 in the final. The following year the cup left the Seven Towers for Coleraine and Stewart was dismissed as manager. His replacement, again as player-manager, was Eddie Russell, who scored in the winning match against Distillery for the County Antrim Shield.

Success, however, was fleeting. The club experienced a massive losing steak when they played a total of thirteen matches, one after the other, without a win. Inevitably the manager was sacked and the job was given to Billy Johnston. The 1978 Irish Cup Final saw Ballymena lose, yet again, to Linfield, 3-1. Excitement mounted when, for the first time ever, Ballymena qualified for the European Cup Winners Cup. Sadly the team lost 3-0 to SK Beveren, twice over.

The following year Alan Campbell took over as manager and the club took the 1981 County Antrim Shield, as well as that year's Irish Cup, beating – yet again – Glentroran, 1-0. Not much happened throughout the 1990s apart from a succession of managers – Jim Hagan, Tommy Jackson, Gary Erwin, Alan Fraser and Nigel Best – and the club was relegated to the First Division in 1995. The team were relegated again in 2001 under manager Kenny Shiels. In 2002 a new 1,800-seater grandstand was built at the Showgrounds and the team were back in top form in 2003, qualifying for the Inter Toto Cup in 2004.

The team is currently being managed by former Northern Ireland goalkeeper, Tommy Wright, and are looking forward to an even brighter future. "United" are generally considered to have one of the biggest and best crowd of supporters, commonly known as the "Sky Blue Army", who follow their team wherever they play. Possibly the club's main sporting rivals are Coleraine FC, while lesser rivals include Larne FC.

Wakehurst Football Club

Forty-one years younger than Ballymena United, the Wakehurst Football Club was set up in 1969 by Francis Smyth, Francis Best and Willie McIlroy. In August of that year the Harryville-based club played their first match against Connor in the first round of the McReynolds Cup, losing 5-3 after the match went into extra time. A few days later, on 14 August, they had their first win, beating Smithfield 2-0.

Memorial Park

The 1971-72 season saw Wakehurst third in the league with several notable wins, including one over the Harryville Amateurs, where the tally was 6-1. A thrilling match against Raceview resulted in no less than nine goals for the Magpies. Newcomer to the team, Garry Erwin, from Ballymena United, scored a whopping five goals in that first game. Wakehurst reached the final of the Junior Shield but lost to previous winners Cromac Albion, 2-0. However, they made up for the loss by taking the Connon Cup, beating the Amateurs after extra time. Wakehurst also deprived the Amateurs of the Toronto Cup after beating their closest neighbours 2-0.

Things improved even more for the club with its new Olympic team, captained by Leo O'Boyle and managed by Brian Craig. This was an incredibly successful team, not losing even one of its 26 league games, as well as taking the O'Kane and Toal Cups.

1980-81 was predominantly the season of Brian Rock and his "Rocky Raiders". They took home four trophies and got to the final of the Irish Junior Cup. Unfortunately they just lost out against Ballynafeigh Methodists. Three successful seasons followed which resulted in Wakehurst deciding to stretch its legs in the Northern Amateur League. They lost their friendly preparation game against Crusaders 4-0 but it was a valuable experience.

The honours handed out for the 1985-86 season included:

Wakehurst Player of the Year:	Pat O' Neill
Young Player Trophy:	Ian Cushenan
Leading Goal-scorer:	Joe Boyle
Olympics Player of the Year:	Pat Jordan
Leading Goal-scorers:	Willie McClean, John Lorimer

At the beginning of 1989-90 there was a change of manager. Brian Rock was obliged to give up his role due to work commitments and was replaced by Joe MacCall. The Olympics had also had a new manager in the shape of Sammy McVicker. Wakehurst went on to win, for a second time, the County Antrim Junior Shield, beating Belfast Rangers 4-1.

There was a lot of change in 2002: Ian Gregg took over as manager and the club entered the League second division. Some fantastic matches followed, including the semi-final against Larne in the County Antrim Shield. The winners, Wakehurst, went on to face Glentoran in the final at the Oval. It was a ferociously well-played game and the final score, 5-0 to Glentoran, doesn't do justice to the Wakehurst effort.

These days the team is managed by Neil Candlish and looks forward to collecting a few more trophies and cups. Home games are played at Ballymena Showgrounds, pitch two, behind the main arena.

St Mary's GAC, Ahoghill

This club was the brainchild of the parish priest, the Reverend Father Henry McGuigan. He called a meeting some time in 1943 to discuss the introduction of Gaelic sports to the small parish and surrounding area. His idea received an enthusiastic response and a committee was promptly elected from the men present; Father McGuigan was President, Patrick McGarry Snr was named Chairman, the Secretary was John Logan, and the Treasurer was Samuel P Haveron. Typically the club had very little in the beginning and were very grateful for the set of sky-blue jerseys which were kindly donated by Ballymena United Football Club. Things greatly improved when, in 1947, Chairman McGarry successfully bid £300 for a playing field; thus St Mary's became the first GAA club in Antrim to purchase its own ground and vest. There followed much success over the next few years, with the club winning several tournaments in Antrim and Derry as well as many "sevens" competitions.

The year 1964 was an important one for the club when they beat

Dwyers in the Junior Championship Final at Casement Park, their first major trophy. In 1972 the club were very proud to watch the official opening of the Father McGuigan Park, ensuring that their founder's name would never be forgotten in Ahoghill.

It is widely believed that the 1973 team was the strongest ever in the club's history. They succeeded in reaching the semi-finals of the Senior Championship but were beaten by Rossa. One of the teams they defeated on the way to the semis were Cargin, who went on to win the championship the following year.

1992 was another good year for the senior football team. They took on Portglenone in the final of the Junior Championship at Rasharkin and beat them 0-9 to 0-5. The team is currently playing at Division Two of the All-County Leagues.

Camogie has always been an important part of the club, with its team, the Camogs, winning the 1948 County Championship and then the Ulster Championship twenty-one years later. After making it to the All-Ireland final they were beaten – just about –by Limerick team, Ahane. The team recently jumped four divisions to Division One in five seasons.

A *hurling* committee was set up in 1974 which formed a juvenile and an adult team. In 1989 the hurling team beat Ballymena to take the Junior Championship at Cushendall. The team now plays in Division Three of the All-County Leagues.

A *juvenile club* was formed in 1978 when St Mary's joined with Portglenone, and it was decided to name it after Sean Stinson, a man who had worked long and hard for the GAA. Beginning in 1995 the football team took four county minor football titles while the under-16 hurlers won two Division Two North Antrim League titles over the last few years. The club strives to improve the standard of under-age hurling, a sport that hasn't received as much attention as Gaelic football and camogie.

In 2003 the club opened the doors to its £200,000

Dundermot Mound

changing/club-room complex, confirming the huge steps it has taken since those lean days of 1943.

Ballymena Golf Club

The Ballymena Golf Club, founded in 1903, is situated approximately two miles north-east of Ballymena, beside the village of Broughshane. The pitch is renowned for the fact it can be played on all year round, thanks to the superb drainage system that ensures its name as the driest inland course in Ireland. Apart from the obvious beauty of the course one can't fail to notice, or enjoy, the spectacle that is Saint Patrick's Slemish which dominates the skyline.

It's a relatively small course at 5,300 metres but scoring is a little more difficult than one expects thanks to well-bunkered greens and no less than six demanding par threes.

Ballymena Rugby Football Club

This club has two beginnings. In 1887 it was first affiliated to the Northern Branch of the Irish Rugby Football Union. However, it really only got going in 1922 when it entered the Junior League for the 1923-24 season, playing its matches at the local Demesne. Over the following decade, before the Second World War, the club had great success, winning the Provincial Towns Cup and the Junior Challenge Cup. There was also a tentative, unsuccessful attempt for the Senior Challenge Cup. After the war, in 1945, the team started playing at the Showgrounds. The new Club President, W.H. Mol, was Headmaster of Ballymena Academy which meant that the players could avail of the academy's changing facilities.

The team went from strength to strength, winning the Junior League Championship in 1950-51, and again in 1951-52. Confidence was growing and an application was made to the Ulster Branch to enter the senior ranks, which was accepted. Ballymena became a Senior Club in time for the 1952-53 season. Two years later they moved to their present address in Eaton Park. At the time the park was a lot smaller at nine acres and the rugby matches were only a minor part of the entertainment on show. Other sports hosted in the park included cricket, tennis, men's hockey and later athletics. The park has since expanded to over thirty acres, complete with pavilion, function hall, grandstand and well-equipped clubhouse.

Meanwhile there was a bit of a lull as far as winning games went, which finally ended in 1962-63 with the taking of the Senior Cup. Then in 1970 Ballymena initiated a squad system and a coaching scheme which resulted in the club's success over the next ten years. The club contributed many fine players to the Ulster Provincial side as well as the Irish International team. In 1980 there was a major club tour to Canada.

Ballymena Internationals who have represented Ireland and Ulster include: Syd Millar, Bill McBride, Barton McCallan, Johnathan Moffett, Ian Dick, Jimmy Dick, Joey Gaston, Robin Gregg, Wallace McMaster, Ian McIlrath, Harry Steele, Trevor Ringland, Steve Smith, Philip Rainey, Brian Robinson, Gordon Hamilton, Derek McAleese, Jonathan Bell, David Humphreys, James Topping, Dion O'Cuinneagain, Gary Longwell, Paul Shields, Matthew McCullough, Andrew Trimble, Bryan Young, Isaac Boss and Pat Wallace. Millar, McBride, Ringland and Smith have also toured with the British Lions.

After the club's centenary Ballymena took the Ulster League and Cup in 1988-89 and 1989-90, and were placed in Division One of the All-Ireland League. In 1996 the club was delighted to welcome on board Nelie Smith as Director of Rugby who implemented changes responsible for an overall improvement in the players' attitude, style of play and fitness levels. As a result the team brought home, for the third time, the Ulster League and Cup double. Smith also attracted several quality players who were eager to benefit from his coaching regime. Smith stayed with the club until 1998. His successor, Andre Bester, took over just before another major tour, of South Africa. Under Bester the club contributed twelve players to the 1999 Ulster team that won the European Cup, a fantastic achievement. Bester's successor was Aussie Tony D'Arcy, from Brisbane, a highly experienced prop for both Australia and Queensland. The highlight of his tenure was when Ballymena beat Clontarf to take the AIL Championship in what was a hugely exciting final at Lansdowne Road in May 2003.

D'Arcy returned to Australia in 2004 and his replacement was South African Steph Nel. After two years Nel left for Cape Town and was replaced by another South African, Jacques Benade, who is with the club on a part-time basis with a three year contract.

PART FOUR
GHOSTS

Lenagh

Like any respectable town, Ballymena has its fair share of things that go bump in the night. And it's not just your average ghosts. Don't forget that before anyone else arrived on this island it was primarily the territory of the – potentially – fearsome fairies of ancient lore. Man had more reason to fear them than anything else.

For instance, when the railway line was being laid between Belfast and Ballymena, sometime in the early 1940s, the workmen came up against what was known to be an old fort with fairy bushes in Lenagh, and it was in the way of progress. The men had their orders: the fort had to be cleared to make way for the railway tracks, but nobody wanted to touch it. After much deliberation and head-scratching one man decided to get on with the job and began to cut away at the outer branches. However, he soon met with an accident, which led to a downing of his workmates' tools. The story goes that the railway officials had no alternative but to blow up the fort, which they did. In its place they found some buried treasure in the form of spearheads and tools. Meanwhile the first workman died from his injuries and, a little while later, the head official became a permanent invalid. A local woman who lived near the fort reported hearing a blood-curdling scream of anger on the evening that the fort was blown up, which she believed came from the fairies being forced to leave their home.

Dundermot Mound

Other strange happenings include the apparition of a four-horse-drawn coach being driven through Dundermot Mound by its ghostly driver. If the spectre spots anyone on the road he will drive up to them to ask, "Is the bridge at Glarryford still up?" The question is deadly because those he asks it of will die within the next twelve months.

Dundermot Mound is also a place where anything that appears remotely demonic must be ignored or avoided altogether. Apparently there is a secret entrance to Hell somewhere in the area which occasionally opens up to release demons who grab any unsuspecting persons and drag them straight down to the fiery pits on a one-way ticket.

The White Gates

One of the most haunted places in Ballymena has to be the Crebilly area. The White Gates can be found on a road just off the Crebilly Road. Just past the gates, down a lane, is an old house whose inhabitants are long gone. It was the scene of a crime which led to a swift death for the perpetrator. Many years ago a horseman stole a large sum of money from the owners of this house – or, at least, he attempted to. He grabbed the cash and jumped on his horse which had been waiting outside. Unfortunately for him the family were able to alert the guards at the gate. A stretch of wire was held high and pulled from one side of the gate to the other by the waiting guards. As the thief rode by at top speed his head was sliced clean from his body. According to locals this man can still be seen, every Hallowe'en, minus his head, riding his horse towards the gates. Some have even reported that they have heard his horse's hooves at midnight thundering down the lane.

The White Gates

Ballymoney

The ghost of George "Bloody" Hutchinsons is a very busy one indeed. Every Friday the 13th, every Hallowe'en, and on every annual anniversary of his death, George has to walk to the bottom of Main Street, turn around and walk back to the top again. Now there is more than one story concerning this ghost. He has been described as walking slowly with a ball and chain around his ankles, and he only makes his journey between midnight and 1am. Some believe that if he fails to finish his walk by 1am his soul will vanish forever, while others believe that anyone who can prevent him from completing his walk will dismiss his spirit for all eternity. His grave is also meant to be a hive of activity on these anniversaries.

Tullyglass Hotel

This sumptuous spot is one of the most popular wedding venues in Northern Ireland. The site dates back to the 1800s and is surrounded by eight acres of gardens and woodlands. It used to be a mansion house and it was during these years that a young girl called Carrie is believed to have died in the tower. Her spirit is said to haunt the hotel to this very day.

Galgorm

In the 1560s the estates of Galgorm were handed by over by James I to the English, High Anglican Colville family, and became known as Mount Colville. A couple of hundred years later, and one of the family's descendants was reputed to be a witch, in league with the Devil himself. The Reverend Alexander Colville was thought to have a library full of books on witchcraft and other things that ordinary, respectable folk had no interest in. Apart from his dubious reading habits he was also known throughout the land for being the worse kind of landlord; he was the type of man who would raise his tenants' rents without a word of warning or any consideration for their plight.

By all accounts he was an immensely unpopular man and, perhaps inevitably, rumours about him spread throughout the surrounding countryside. Some believed him to be a devil-worshipper; others said that he had a magic mirror which allowed him to watch events in places as far away as London; tales were told of his invisibility which permitted him to rob his already poor tenants, so that when he increased their rents they would definitely be unable to pay what was owed, and could be evicted. The mean landlord was blamed for any mishaps that befell the people on his land or those who knew him. Locals were convinced that he could cast spells and raise demons that could bring about sickness and even death.

There is one story in particular which has been passed down from generation to generation concerning the Reverend which concerns the selling of his soul to the Devil to get out of a financial fix. Once the payment had been made, in the form of a lot of gold, the Devil informed the Reverend that he would be back for his soul in thirteen years time. When he returned after the allotted time he found the landlord reading his Bible by the light of one candle. Of course, it was well known that the Devil could not approach a man when the Bible was open, and the Reverend informed the Prince of Darkness that he'd be with him as soon as the candle burnt out. When the Devil accepted this, Colville blew out the candle and put it between the pages of the Bible where the Devil couldn't reach it, saying that since the candle could never burn itself out the deal was now off. The Devil left in a rage. However it was all just a matter of time.

A few months later, while the Reverend was away, his servant found the stub of the candle in the Bible and lit it. When the candle, finally, burnt out a loud evil laugh was heard throughout the castle. The landlord knew what had happened as soon as he returned home. He quickly hatched a plan to hold on to his miserable soul. The date for the exchange was 28 February, so he made sure that he spent that entire day in prayer with the Bible by his side. Once the day was over,

Colville went back to the whiskey, gambling and whatever else he preferred to do instead of praying. For the next few years he managed to escape settling his debt with the Devil until one fateful day when he made a fatal error. After a day of hymn-singing and Bible reading, the Reverend was back on the hard stuff once the clock struck midnight to mark the end of another 28 February. Unfortunately, Colville was completely oblivious to the fact that this particular year was a leap year. Another servant answered a loud knocking on the castle's door and presented a tall, dark visitor who promptly threw his cloak around the stricken Reverend. Neither of them was ever seen again.

It is said that the Devil patrols the grounds of the castle today as a massive, red-eyed hound while the Reverend Colville has been spotted in the gardens standing over the sun-dial, presumably checking the precise date and time. The church – the meeting place of the Devil and the landlord – is still there, and legend has it that the "soul-less" body of Colville is buried in a tomb underneath the altar. This tomb is a veritable "no-go" area, especially after dark.

Galgorm Castle Crypt

SUGGESTED WEBSITES

www.ahoghillgaa.com
www.ballymenagolfclub.co.uk
www.ballymenarfc.com
www.ballymenaroadclub.couk
www.ballymenaunitedfc.com
www.ballymena.gov.uk
www.thecanadianencyclopedia.com
www.causewaycoastandglens.com
www.cccdisciples.org
www.christianitytoday.com
www.cr.nps.gov
www.davidwilliams.com
www.freewebs.com
www.greenfeesavers.co.uk
www.hypertexts.com
www.mstreetgallery.com
www.newadvent.org
www.news.bbc.co.uk
www.painterkeys.com
www.paranormaldatabase.com
www.pgil-eirdata.org
www.schenectadyhistory.org
www.restorationmovement.info
www.theshadowlands.net
www.triskelle.eu
www.ulsterbiography.co.uk
www.ulsterhistory.com
www.wakehurstfc.co.uk

BIBLIOGRAPHY

Andrew W Allen, *Joe Craig*, Ballymena Borough Council, 1994

Jonathan Bardon, *A History of Ulster*, The Blackstaff Press, 2001

Bob Curran, *A Bewitched Land, Ireland's Witches*, The O'Brien Press, 2005

Bob Curran, *North Antrim Seven Towers to Nine Glens*, Cottage Publications, 2005

Eull Dunlop, Jack Dunlop and Sandy Kernohan, *Ahoghill Folk Park Two*, Mid-Antrim Historical Group, 1989

Eull Dunlop, *Ballymena Sketches & Recollections*, Mid-Antrim Historical Group, 1992

Eull Dunlop, *Ballymena Town Hall 1928 and Other Aspects of Civil History*, Braid Books, 1984

Dean Hayes, *Northern Ireland's Greats 100 Top Football Heroes*, Appletree Press, Belfast, 2005

Brian Lalor, *The Encyclopaedia of Ireland*, Gill & Macmillan, 2003

Daragh O'Halloran, *Green Beat: The Forgotten Era of Irish Rock*, Brehon Press, Belfast, 2006

Maurice O'Neill, *Ballymena An Illustrated History and Companion*, Cottage Publications, 1994

Unknown, *Industries of the North One Hundred Years Ago*, The Friar's Bush Press, 1986

Unknown, *Old Ballymena: A History of Ballymena during the 1798 Rebellion*

Christopher Winn, *I Never Knew That About Ireland*, Ebury Press, 2006

INDEX

A

Adair, Robert, 18, 21

Adair, Robert Alexander Shafto, 30, 37

Adair, William, 17, 18

Ahoghill, 40

American Declaration of Independence, 25

Archer, Thomas, 28

"Armed Science", 38

Arthur, Chester Alan, 53

B

Ballykeel, 14

Ballymena Academy, 22

Ballymena Castle, 30

Ballymena Golf Club, 140

Ballymena Observer, 12, 29, 49

Ballymena Poor Law Union, 34

Ballymena Road Club, 129

Ballymena Rugby Club, 140

Ballymena Times, 30

Ballymena United, 132

Ballymena Workhouse, 34

Battle of the Boyne, 18

Battle of Tawnybrack, 16

Belfast and Ballymena Railway, 33

Belfast News Letter, 25, 45

Bell, Alexander Graham, 54

Bell, John, 38

Braidwater Spinning Mill, 34

Broughshane, 45

Bruce, Edward, 16

Bruce, Robert, 16

C

Campbell, Alexander, 58

    The Christian Baptist, 61

    The Christian System on the Remission of Sins, 62

    The Living Oracles, 62

    The Millennial Harbinger, 62

Camphill Fort, 14

Carbery, Ethna, 62

    In The Celtic Past, 65

    The Four Winds of Éireann, 65

    The Northern Patriot, 64

    The Passionate Hearts, 65

    Shan Van Vocht, 64

Carson, John & Son, 38

Casement, Sir Roger, 114

Cennick, John, 22

Chaucer, *Canterbury Tales*, 17

Cleveland, Grover, 65

Clough, 44
Cochrane, Ian, 73
    A Streak of Madness, 74
    Gone In The Head, 74
Colfin Glen, 17
Columbus, Christopher, 25
Colville, Reverend Alexander, 148
Connolly, James, 113
Craig, Joe, 76
Cullybackey, 41

D

Davis, Steven, 80
Dean, Joseph, 22
de Burgo, Richard, 16
de Courcy, John, 14, 16
Degan, Bishop, 14
Duke of York, 38
Dundermot Mound, 146
Dunskey Castle, 18

E

Eaton, Timothy, 81

F

Fairhill Shopping Centre, 18
Faneilli, Giuseppi, 117
fitz Audelin, William, 16
Fitzgerald, Robert, 17
Forsythe, Graham, 84

G

Galgorm Castle, 21
Gault Brothers, 32
Gault, John, 33
Geronimo, 70
Gibraltar, 49
Glenravel, 42

Goldman, Emma, 118
Gracehill Moravian Settlement, 22, 45
Grant, President Ulysses S, 53
Great fire of London, 20
Great plague of London, 20
Guevara, Ernet "Che", 80
Guiteau, Charles Julius, 54

H

Hanna, John, 33
Hus, John, 22
Hutchinsons, George "Bloody", 148

J

Johnson, Samuel, 25
Joy, Francis, 25

K

Kane Brothers, 32
Kells and Connor, 41
Kennedy, Walter, 18
King Charles I, 18
King Geoge II, 26
King Henry II, 16
King Louis XVI, 26
King William III, 21
Kinhilt Castle, 18
Kirkinriola, 14

L

Lanyon, Charles, 33
Lenagh, 144
Loughrane, Eamonn, 86
Lynn, John, 86

M

Marie Antoinette, 26

Melville, Herman, *Moby Dick*, 29

Memorial Park, 49

McAteer, Archibald & family, 49

McBride, Sean, 116

McBride, William John, 88

McCartney, David and Son, 32

McCartney, Samuel J, 32

McCaughren, Tom, 89

    Run For Cover, 92

    Run To Earth, 92

    Run Swift, Run Free, 92

    Run To The Ark, 92

    Run To The Wild Wood, 92

    Run With The Wind, 92

McCorley, Roddy, 65

McCracken, Henry Joy, 25, 28

McHenry, James, 92

McTurk, Samuel, 38

McWilliams, David, 94

    "The Days of Pearly Spencer", 97

Millar, Syd, 97

Milligan, Alice, 64

M'keen, Bab, *Bab M'Keen's Almanac*, 29

Moorfields, 44

Morton, Robert and Co., 32

Murdock, Colin, 98

N

Neeson, Liam, 100

Norton, John Lansdowne, 80

O

Óg MacQuillan, Ruairí, 17

Oldstone Castle, 20

O'Neill, Charles, 46

O'Neill, Shane, 17

P

Paisley, Ian, 102

Parish Church of Saint Patrick, 14, 21

Parnell, Charles Stewart, 62

Peacock, Sir Thomas, 46

People's Park, 37

Peters, Mary, 105

Portglenone, 40

Poynz, John, 38

Q

Queen Elizabeth I, 16

R

Raphael, James, 28

1798 Rebellion, 26

Reeves, Rector William, 21

Restoration Movement, 60

Ringforts, 14

Royal Iniskilling Fusiliers, 48

Royal Irish Rangers, 48

Royal Irish Regiment, 48

Royal Ulster Rifles, 46, 48

S

Saint Patrick, 12, 106

Saint Patrick's Barracks, 46

Sequah, the healer, 109

Seven towers, 37

Simms, Robert A, 33

Slemish, 12

Smith, Sir Thomas, 16

St Mary's GAC, 137

Straney, John, 116

T
Thatch Inn, 45
Tullyglass Hotel, 148
Turpin, Dick, 26
Twain, Mark, 57

U
Ulster Linen Board, 45

V
Viscount Massereene, 10th, 33

W
Wakehurst Football Club, 134
Waveney, Lord, 22, 37
Weir, John, 29
Wesley, John, 22
White Gates, 146
White, Jack, 112
White Knight, 17
Wilson, George S, 32
Worthington, Nigel, 122
Wright, Alexander, 124
Württemburg, Duke of, 21
Wylie, John, 42